I0831077

MATCHA

抹茶

INDEX

WELCOME TO THE WORLD OF MATCHA

FOR ME, A NICE, WARM CUP OF TEA has always been more than just a simple drink. It's a beautiful opportunity to gather loved ones around the table and enjoy precious moments. It is also a perfect conversation starter; it brings family and friends together and creates lasting memories. These beloved traditions remind me of small joys in life and the importance of connection with myself and those I care about.

But I realized that this simple ritual, which I deeply cherish, could go way beyond that. By exploring new flavors and healthier options, I discovered matcha, which elevated my tea experience to new heights. I found that a cup of tea could be way more than just a comforting beverage—it can become a new lifestyle and a secure path towards good health and greater mindfulness. By incorporating this finely ground powder into my diet, I became more aware of my body and mind and the profound impact it had on my overall well-being.

And I'm not the only one! In recent years, more and more people are replacing their regular tea with matcha. This vibrant drink has gained immense popularity worldwide, becoming a staple for those seeking to improve their daily routines. Everyone, from wellness enthusiasts and health experts to tea lovers, seems to be captivated by this powerful drink and its mind-blowing properties. No wonder!

Matcha has the power to heal our bodies from within, which is especially important nowadays, given our modern lifestyles, poor dietary choices, and the rise of chronic diseases. It's becoming more and more difficult to achieve and maintain the health and wellness we want, as the fast pace of life leaves little room for mindful self-care, and many conventional approaches only address symptoms rather than root causes. In such times, we often lean toward unnatural quantities of pharmaceuticals, which may or may not be effective, weakening our immune systems and impacting our overall health.

This is why I genuinely believe we have no choice but to forge our path to wellness by adopting simple yet powerful routines and incorporating this ancient health elixir into our daily lives. This simple, nutrient-rich superfood could help us reclaim balance and guide us back to the path of long-term well-being. That was the birth of the idea for this book. I wanted to create something that provides people with knowledge about this effective superfood and helps them regain their health through a practical strategy for incorporating matcha into their lives.

Whether you decide to enjoy it as a latte, in smoothies, or bake into treats, matcha's versatility is something you simply can't ignore. It's one of the best superfoods for well-being and health—it boosts metabolism, enhances focus and calmness, and supports heart health and weight loss. With its rich composition and unique earthy flavor, matcha is not only healthy but also a fantastic ingredient that can easily be added to various recipes, making it a true nutrient powerhouse for the entire family. Furthermore, it's an excellent way to add a little twist to your favorite recipes, giving them an extra kick of flavor and nutrition that everybody will enjoy.

This book aims to help you discover this powerful superfood and unlock its outstanding health benefits, which can easily fit into your diet. It will take you on a journey through the rich history and cultural importance of matcha, its amazing health benefits, and culinary versatility. Along the way, you'll also find practical tips and simple recipes to help you incorporate matcha into your everyday routine and improve the overall health and well-being of you and your loved ones.

INTRODUCTION TO MATCHA

IF YOU'RE SOMEONE WHO IS CONCERNED WITH WELLNESS AND HEALTHY living and looking for something new to add to your diet, chances are you've already heard about matcha. Most likely, you tried matcha in the form of tea, latte, or smoothie in your local café; you enjoyed the flavor, and now you're on the hunt for more recipes and ways to consume matcha daily. Most importantly, you want to be healthy, energized, and focused throughout the day. After all, that's the number one driving force for most people to start incorporating powerful superfoods, such as matcha, into their lifestyle.

In this chapter, I will explain what makes matcha so special. Together, we'll explore the unique process of how it's grown, harvested, and transformed into a fine powder. This process is key to understanding both the taste and nutritional benefits that set matcha apart from other types of green tea. It's what makes matcha a worldwide trendy drink and a valuable addition to your everyday diet. Let's dig in...

世界で一番のお茶

NO. 1 TEA IN THE WORLD

Why did matcha gain such popularity? Apart from its intense color and amazing flavor, matcha's benefits lie in its distinctive preparation, which preserves a far greater amount of nutrients than most other methods.

WHEN YOU PREPARE TRADITIONAL GREEN TEA, the leaves are steeped in hot water, and the water-soluble nutrients are extracted before the leaves are discarded. With matcha, however, the entire tea leaf is consumed in powdered form, meaning you're ingesting the full range of antioxidants, vitamins, and minerals the leaf has to offer. This unique preparation is what makes matcha tea so special, and health experts often advise this type of tea. It's also what gives matcha its special flavor, which pairs perfectly with various other foods.

What's remarkable about matcha isn't just its flavor and color but also the potential health benefits packed into each cup. Because you're consuming the whole leaf rather than an infusion, matcha is a more potent source of antioxidants, especially catechins, such as epigallocatechin gallate (EGCG). This powerful antioxidant has amazing anti-inflammatory properties that are essential for preventing chronic diseases and improving overall health. What's more, EGCG can help boost your metabolism, which is important for maintaining healthy weight and muscle mass. Simply put, matcha takes what's already good about green tea and significantly amplifies it.

About three weeks before harvest, matcha tea plants are covered to shield them from direct sunlight.

But the magic of matcha goes beyond the antioxidants. One of the compounds that make matcha unique is L-theanine, an amino acid that works to promote relaxation without causing drowsiness. This means that matcha doesn't just offer a typical caffeine boost; instead, it provides what many describe as a "calm alertness." The L-theanine in matcha helps control the jittery feelings that you may experience from caffeine. This is why people who drink matcha daily often feel more focused and have energy that lasts the whole day. But we'll get back to the science behind matcha later...

Now, let's talk a bit more about how matcha is grown and why that matters for both flavor and nutrition. Matcha comes from the same plant as all green teas—Camellia sinensis. However, the cultivation process is what makes all the difference.

About three weeks before harvest, matcha tea plants are covered to shield them from direct sunlight. This shading encourages the plants to produce more chlorophyll and amino

Matcha comes from the same plant as all green teas—Camellia sinensis.

acids, which not only deepens matcha's iconic bright green color but also contributes to its unique flavor. This careful cultivation gives matcha its smooth, rich taste, far more complex than typical green teas.

The shading process plays a crucial role in altering the chemical composition of the tea leaves. Chlorophyll, the pigment responsible for the green color, increases significantly, giving matcha its vibrant appearance. But it's not just about aesthetics. Chlorophyll has detoxifying properties that help your body eliminate toxins and promote overall well-being. Matcha is often regarded as a natural detoxifier, making it a popular choice for those seeking a holistic approach to health.

After the harvest, only the youngest and most tender leaves are selected for the highest-quality matcha. The leaves are then steamed to stop oxidation. This process ensures matcha retains its vibrant color and an entire spectrum of nutrients. After that, matcha leaves are dried, and the stems and veins are removed. What remains is known as tencha, which is stone-ground into the fine powder we know as matcha. This traditional grinding process is often done slowly over several hours, but it is essential for creating the smooth, velvety texture of high-quality matcha that will keep its maximum nutritional value.

For many people—myself included—matcha can be a bit of an acquired taste. However, its extraordinary benefits make it well worth exploring. The truth is that the flavor is distinct but good. People often describe it as earthy, slightly sweet, with a hint of bitterness. What sets matcha apart from other green teas in terms of flavor is its perfect balance of natural bitterness and sweetness. It is precisely this balance that makes matcha so versatile. You can enjoy it traditionally with just water, or you can experiment by adding it to lattes, smoothies, or even baked goods for a unique twist.

For those new to matcha, it's worth mentioning that not all matcha is created equal. The two main matcha tea grades are further divided into five grades. The highest quality matcha, known as a ceremonial grade, is typically used for traditional tea ceremonies and is characterized by its vibrant color and smooth taste. Culinary-grade matcha, on the other hand, is slightly more bitter and used primarily for cooking or adding to beverages, such as smoothies or lattes. It's important to know the difference so you can select the right type for your needs. Ceremonial matcha is best enjoyed on its own, while culinary matcha can be a great addition to various recipes. But we'll talk more about it later.

YOU CAN ENJOY IT TRADITIONALLY WITH JUST WATER, OR YOU CAN EXPERIMENT BY ADDING IT TO LATTES, SMOOTHIES, OR EVEN BAKED GOOD

Let's get back to matcha's outstanding health benefits because that's why we're here, right? As I said earlier, regular consumption of matcha has been linked to a range of health benefits, from supporting heart health to aiding in weight management. Furthermore, the catechins in matcha help protect cells from damage caused by free radicals, which can reduce the risk of chronic diseases, such as cancer and heart disease.

If that wasn't good enough, matcha is also rich in other important nutrients, including vitamins A, C, and E, and minerals such as potassium and magnesium. These vitamins and minerals support various bodily functions, such as boosting the immune system and promoting healthy skin. When consumed regularly, matcha can help improve overall health and well-being, making it a valuable addition to any diet.

The possibilities for incorporating matcha into your daily routine are endless. While matcha tea is the most common way of consuming this superfood, you can also add matcha powder to a variety of recipes. From smoothies and lattes to baked goods and savory dishes, matcha's versatility in the kitchen makes it easy to enjoy in many different ways.

The calmness and surroundings are a big part of the matcha experience. Make sure to enjoy your matcha in a peaceful setting to achieve the best matcha experience.

If you're looking to start your day with an energy boost, a matcha latte made with almond milk and a touch of honey can be a delicious and nutritious option. Or, if you prefer a post-workout snack, matcha energy balls made with nuts, dates, and coconut are a great way to refuel. Matcha can also be incorporated into more creative recipes, such as matcha-infused pancakes or salad dressings. Its slightly earthy flavor pairs well with a range of ingredients, allowing you to experiment and find what works best for your taste. For this reason, I have decided to share with you some of my favorite matcha recipes, which can be easily incorporated into your daily menu.

Finally, I have to note that while matcha offers many health benefits, it's always best to consume it in moderation. Like all sources of caffeine, matcha can cause adverse effects, such as jitteriness or insomnia, if consumed in large amounts. However, because of its balanced combination of caffeine and L-theanine, matcha generally provides a more even and sustained energy boost compared with coffee, making it a great alternative for those who are sensitive to caffeine's stronger effects.

As you explore the world of matcha, remember that its benefits go beyond physical health. The practice of preparing and drinking matcha can also be a meditative experience, promoting mindfulness and relaxation. In traditional Japanese tea ceremonies, the preparation of matcha is done with great care and attention to detail, creating a sense of calm and focus. Even if you're just whisking up a quick matcha latte at home, taking a moment to appreciate the process can be a simple but effective way to bring mindfulness into your day.

抹茶

THE HISTORY OF MATCHA

Health experts today recognize this powerful superfood and its mind-blowing benefits, but the story of matcha is so much more than that. This vibrant tea is deeply rooted in ancient cultures and centuries-old traditions, making matcha an inimitable part of human history.

The Beginnings in Ancient China

The story of matcha starts in China during the Tang Dynasty (618–907 CE). At the time, tea was an essential part of daily life, and its preparation was far different from what we know today. Instead of brewing loose leaves, the Chinese developed a method of steaming and compressing tea leaves into bricks. These tea bricks were convenient for trade and easy to transport over long distances. When people wanted to enjoy tea, they would break off a piece of the brick, grind it into powder, and whisk it with hot water; this early method bears a striking resemblance to the matcha we know today. Although this powdered tea gained popularity in China, it was in Japan where matcha truly found its home and began to evolve into the drink we now love.

Pagoda in the Sui and Tang Dynasties National Historical Park, Luoyang, Henan, China

The Journey to Japan

In the 12th century, Zen Buddhist monks from Japan traveled to China to study and brought back tea seeds and the method of preparing powdered tea. One monk in particular, Myoan Eisai, is often credited with introducing matcha to Japan. He discovered that matcha could do more than just quench thirst—it had a calming effect that helped monks during long meditation sessions. The slow, mindful process of whisking the tea also became a meditative practice in itself.

Matcha soon became an integral part of Zen Buddhist culture. Due to its unique combination of caffeine and L-theanine, matcha allowed the monks to stay alert yet calm during hours of meditation. This balance helped monks enhance their focus, deepen their mindfulness, and embrace the calm, meditative state.

As matcha spread throughout Japan, it began to capture the attention of another group—the samurai. Samurai were Japanese elite warriors known for their discipline and honor. Before going to war, they would drink matcha to help sharpen their minds and deepen their focus. This is how matcha became a symbol of physical and mental strength all over Japan.

For the samurai, drinking matcha was more than just getting energy—it was about strengthening the body and mind and preparing for the challenges ahead. This sense of ritual and respect for the tea would later become a hallmark of the traditional Japanese tea ceremony.

The Japanese Tea Ceremony (Chanoyu)

One of the most beautiful and enduring aspects of matcha culture in Japan is unquestionably the tea ceremony, known as chanoyu (meaning "the way of tea"). This ceremonial preparation and consumption of matcha is more than just a way to drink tea—it's a spiritual and cultural practice that has been passed down through generations.

The tea ceremony is deeply rooted in Japanese culture and reflects four key elements: harmony (wa), respect (kei), purity (sei), and tranquility (jaku). Each movement during the ceremony is performed with grace and mindfulness, from the careful scooping of the matcha powder to the slow, deliberate whisking. The host prepares the tea as an offering of respect and hospitality to their guests, and each guest drinks the matcha in a manner that shows gratitude and appreciation.

What's remarkable about chanoyu is its emphasis on the present moment. This entire experience is meant to invoke a sense of peace and connection with yourself and your surroundings.

Matcha's Cultural Significance in Japan

Over the centuries and up until today, matcha has become a beloved part of Japanese culture. It is more than just a drink; matcha is a symbol of Japanese culture and values. Apart from being the center of the Japanese tea ceremony, it has found its place in everyday life. This vibrant tea represents a sense of calmness amid the chaos of daily life and people's connection to nature and themselves.

While traditional tea ceremonies are still practiced, matcha has also found its way into modern cuisine. From matcha-flavored sweets and desserts to matcha lattes and ice cream, this vibrant green tea is now enjoyed in countless ways. It has transcended its origins in Buddhist monasteries and samurai households to become a widely appreciated ingredient in contemporary Japanese food and drink.

Matcha in Modern Times

In recent years, matcha has claimed its well-earned global recognition. This fantastic tea is praised for its health benefits and versatility. While its roots are steeped in ancient tradition, matcha has adapted to modern tastes and lifestyles. Whether sipped in a quiet tea room, blended into a smoothie, or whisked into a trendy matcha latte, this powdered green tea continues to inspire and nourish people around the world.

What makes matcha so special is its ability to bridge the old and the new. Its rich history reminds us of the spiritual and mindful practices of the past, while its growing popularity today shows us how timeless its benefits truly are. Whether you're drawn to matcha for its calming effects, its vibrant flavor, or its numerous health benefits, there's no denying that matcha's legacy is as strong as ever.

As we move forward, matcha remains a symbol of balance, mindfulness, and connection—a bridge between the ancient and the modern, the physical and the spiritual. And now, as you explore this book and discover new ways to enjoy matcha, you're becoming a part of that history, too.

抹茶の裏側
科学

THE SCIENCE BEHIND MATCHA

Matcha is loaded with nutrients, many of which offer incredible health benefits. It's well known for its abundance of antioxidants, specifically catechins.

ANTIOXIDANTS ARE MOLECULES that protect your body from oxidative stress caused by free radicals: unstable molecules that can damage cells and lead to chronic diseases, such as cancer, heart disease, and aging-related conditions. The catechins in matcha, particularly EGCG, have been extensively studied for their cancer-fighting properties. Furthermore, EGCG has been shown to not only combat free radicals but also reduce inflammation in the body, which can lower the risk of chronic diseases. It's this high concentration of antioxidants that makes matcha particularly effective at protecting your cells from oxidative damage, helping to keep your body functioning at its best.

However, antioxidants aren't the only impressive feature of matcha. This green tea powder is also rich in L-theanine, an amino acid that plays a key role in its calming yet energizing effects. L-theanine works by increasing the production of alpha waves in the brain, which are associated with a state of relaxed alertness. So, unlike the jittery energy boost you may get from coffee, matcha provides a more balanced energy and promotes a calm, focused state of mind. In other words, while caffeine stimulates the brain and increases alertness, L-theanine counteracts the jittery effects, allowing you to stay focused and relaxed at the same time. This unique combination of caffeine and L-theanine makes matcha an ideal drink for those who want to stay alert and productive without the anxiety or crashes that often come with other caffeinated beverages.

Additionally, matcha is packed with a variety of vitamins and minerals that contribute to its overall health benefits. It's a great source of vitamins A, C, E, and K, which are essential for maintaining healthy skin, supporting the immune system, and promoting blood clotting and bone health. The minerals in matcha, such as potassium, calcium, and iron, help support various bodily functions, including regulating blood pressure, strengthening bones, and preventing anemia.

VITAMIN C

GOOD FOR YOUR IMMUNE SYSTEM AND WRINKLES

Vitamin C is well known for its immunity-boosting properties, and matcha is a good source of this vital nutrient. It helps your body fend off illnesses by strengthening the immune system and supporting the production of white blood cells, which are key defenders against infections. Vitamin C also acts as an antioxidant, neutralizing free radicals and reducing oxidative stress. This not only helps fight off harmful pathogens but also contributes to youthful-looking skin by promoting collagen production. Collagen is essential for skin elasticity, and sufficient levels of vitamin C can help prevent wrinkles and other signs of aging.

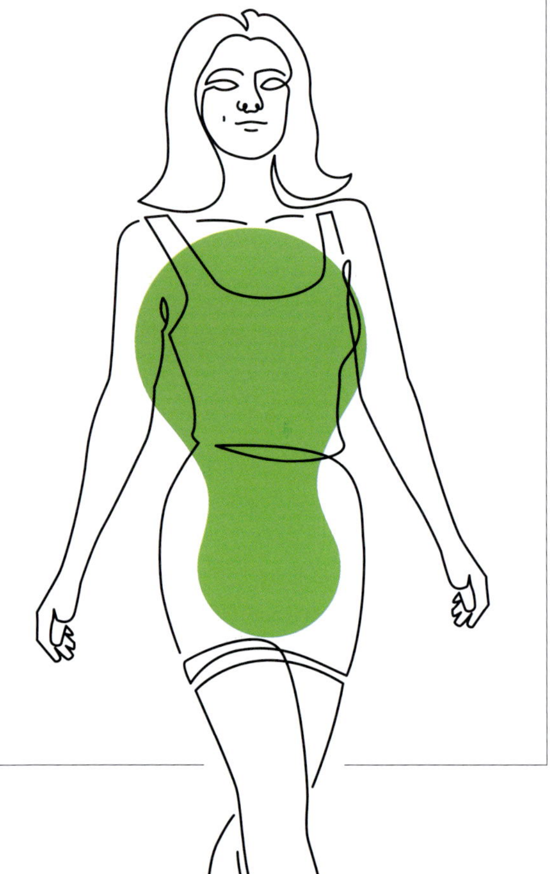

VITAMIN A

GOOD FOR YOUR EYES, SKIN AND IMMUNE SYSTEM

Matcha contains a notable amount of vitamin A, which is crucial for maintaining healthy vision. Vitamin A plays an important role in the health of your eyes by supporting the retina's function and helping with night vision. In addition to eye health, this vitamin also helps maintain healthy skin and boosts the immune system. Vitamin A is essential for cell growth and regeneration, meaning it can also promote faster healing of skin and tissues.

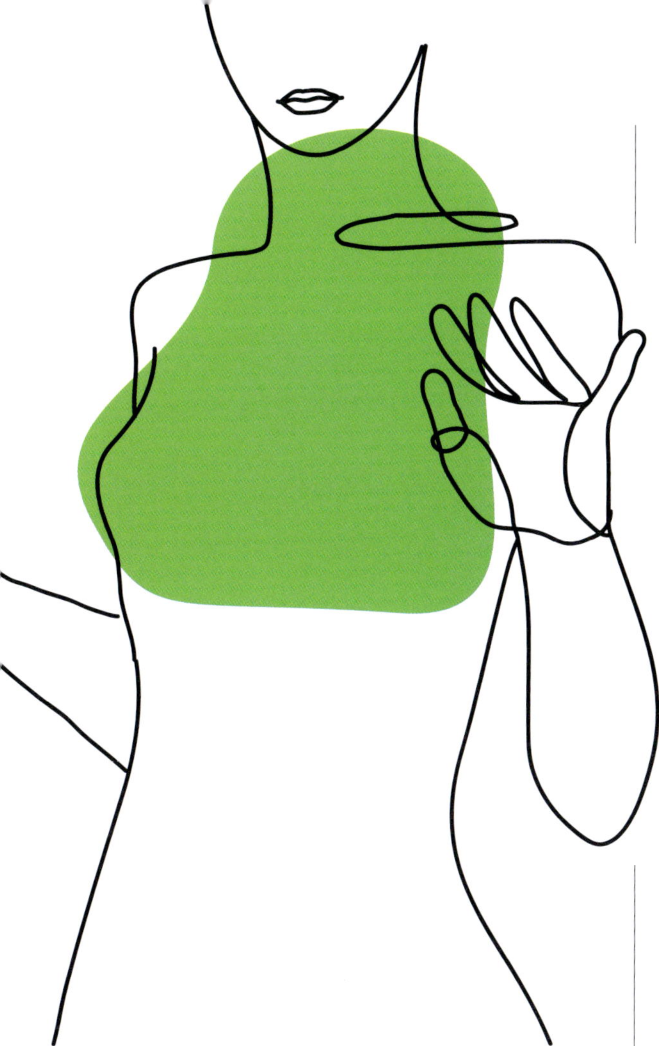

VITAMIN E

GOOD FOR PROTECTING YOUR SKIN

Another powerful antioxidant found in matcha is vitamin E, which plays a significant role in protecting your cells from oxidative damage. By neutralizing harmful free radicals, vitamin E helps protect your skin from damage caused by environmental stressors, such as ultraviolet rays and pollution. It also supports skin health by moisturizing and maintaining the integrity of skin cells, making your skin look more radiant and youthful. Beyond skincare, vitamin E contributes to a healthy immune system and helps your body repair damaged tissues.

VITAMIN K

GOOD FOR YOUR HEALING WOUNDS AND BONES

Vitamin K is essential for blood clotting, which means it helps your body heal wounds properly and prevents excessive bleeding. This vitamin is also important for maintaining strong bones, as it plays a role in calcium regulation. By supporting calcium binding in bones and tissues, vitamin K helps prevent bone disorders, such as osteoporosis, and keeps your skeleton strong as you age. Including matcha in your diet can provide a boost to your bone health and ensure that your body has the necessary nutrients to repair and strengthen itself.

MAGNESIUM

GOOD FOR YOUR MUSCLE FUNCTION, NERVE TRANSMISSION, AND MAINTAINING A HEALTHY HEART RHYTHM

Magnesium is one of the standout minerals in matcha, playing a key role in hundreds of biochemical reactions in the body. It is essential for muscle function, nerve transmission, and maintaining a healthy heart rhythm. Magnesium also contributes to bone health by working alongside calcium to build strong bones. Beyond that, it helps regulate blood sugar levels and supports energy production, making it vital for reducing fatigue. For those struggling with stress or insomnia, magnesium has calming properties that can help relax muscles and improve sleep quality.

POTASSIUM

GOOD FOR MAINTAINING FLUID BALANCE AND SUPPORTING HEALTHY BLOOD PRESSURE LEVELS

Potassium is an electrolyte that is crucial for maintaining fluid balance in the body and supporting healthy blood pressure levels. It works to counteract the effects of sodium, which can elevate blood pressure, making potassium important for cardiovascular health. Additionally, potassium plays a vital role in proper muscle function and nerve signaling. Whether you're exercising or just going about your day, potassium helps ensure that your muscles contract smoothly and your nervous system functions efficiently. Including matcha in your diet gives you a natural source of potassium, which helps maintain proper heart function and prevent muscle cramps.

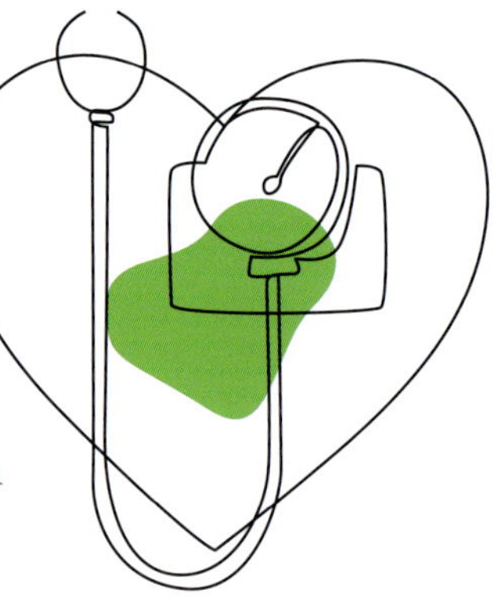

CALCIUM

GOOD FOR YOUR TEETH

Though matcha isn't as famous for its calcium content as dairy products, it still provides a valuable source of this mineral. Calcium is, of course, most well-known for building and maintaining strong bones and teeth. However, it's also essential for muscle contractions, blood clotting, and ensuring that nerves send signals properly. As we age, our calcium needs increase, making it even more important to incorporate calcium-rich foods and drinks, such as matcha, into your routine. By regularly consuming matcha, you help support your bone density and reduce the risk of conditions such as osteoporosis.

IRON

GOOD FOR YOUR ENERGY

Iron is essential for the production of hemoglobin, the protein in red blood cells that carries oxygen throughout the body. Adequate iron levels are important for maintaining energy, preventing fatigue, and ensuring that your muscles and tissues receive enough oxygen to function properly. While matcha doesn't provide as much iron as meat or legumes, it still offers a plant-based source that contributes to your daily iron intake. This is particularly helpful for those who follow a vegetarian or vegan diet and may need additional sources of non-heme iron to prevent anemia.

ZINC

GOOD FOR YOUR IMMUNE SYSTEM

Zinc is another mineral found in matcha, and although it's present only in small amounts, it's still significant for various bodily functions. Zinc is critical for immune function, helping your body fend off infections and heal wounds quickly. It also plays a role in DNA synthesis, cell division, and protein synthesis, meaning it's vital for growth and repair throughout the body. Additionally, zinc supports skin health, promoting a clearer complexion and helping to prevent acne. Having matcha in your diet can contribute to meeting your daily zinc needs, aiding in overall immune defense and skin maintenance.

PHOSPHORUS

GOOD FOR YOUR BONES AND TEETH

Phosphorus is another important mineral found in matcha, working closely with calcium to maintain healthy bones and teeth. In addition to bone health, phosphorus plays a crucial role in how the body uses carbohydrates and fats. It's also involved in the production of energy and the creation of proteins for the growth, maintenance, and repair of cells and tissues. By ensuring you get enough phosphorus, you support your body's ability to produce energy efficiently, which helps keep you feeling alert and active.

CHROMIUM

GOOD FOR YOUR ENERGY LEVELS AND BLOOD SUGAR

Chromium is a trace mineral found in matcha that is often overlooked but plays an important role in regulating blood sugar levels. It enhances the action of insulin, a hormone that's key in the metabolism of carbohydrates, fats, and proteins. For those who are looking to maintain steady energy levels throughout the day and avoid sugar crashes, chromium helps by improving your body's ability to manage glucose effectively. While matcha's chromium content is not large, it's still a helpful addition to your overall mineral intake for balanced energy.

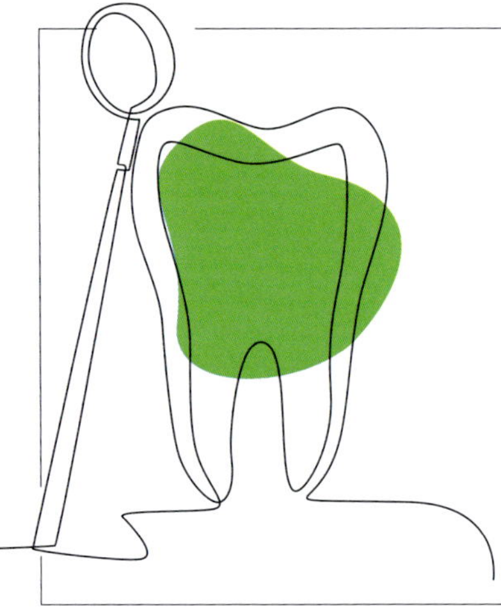

FLUORIDE

GOOD FOR YOUR TOOTH ENAMEL AND PREVENTING CAVITIES

Fluoride, which is often associated with dental care, is naturally found in matcha and can help support oral health by strengthening tooth enamel and preventing cavities. Fluoride's role in mineralizing bones and teeth makes it an important component for long-term dental health. Sipping on matcha can give your teeth an extra layer of defense against decay while you enjoy its other health benefits.

COPPER

GOOD FOR YOUR RED BLOOD CELLS

Copper is a trace mineral present in matcha, playing a role in producing red blood cells and maintaining healthy nerve cells and immune function. Copper also aids in the absorption of iron, ensuring that your body gets the maximum benefit from iron-rich foods or supplements. Additionally, copper supports the formation of collagen, which is crucial for the health of your skin and connective tissues. Though we only need small amounts of copper, it is essential for overall metabolic health.

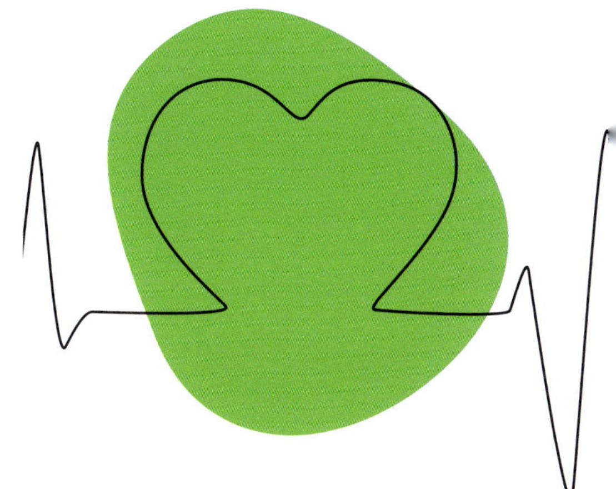

THE IMPORTANCE OF THESE MINERALS TOGETHER

One of the unique attractions of matcha is that it offers a blend of these essential minerals, making it a well-rounded source of nutrition. When consumed regularly, these minerals work together to support everything from energy metabolism and muscle function to bone health and immune response. Because matcha is consumed as a whole-leaf powder, you're getting a more concentrated form of these minerals compared with steeped green tea.

DETOXIFYING EFFECTS OF CHLOROPHYLL

GOOD FOR YOUR SKIN HEALTH, DIGESTION AND OVERALL WELLNESS

Another standout component of matcha is its high chlorophyll content, which gives it a unique green color. Chlorophyll is not only responsible for the plant's color but it also offers detoxifying benefits for the body. When consumed, chlorophyll helps to bind with toxins, heavy metals, and other harmful chemicals, aiding in their elimination from the body.

The detoxifying effects of chlorophyll can lead to improved skin health, better digestion, and overall wellness. Many people find that drinking matcha regularly helps clear up their skin, reduces bloating, and leaves them feeling more energized. The detox process also supports liver function, which plays a crucial role in your body's ability to cleanse itself of harmful substances.

抹茶の健康効果

HEALTH BENEFITS OF MATCHA

From its striking detoxifying properties to its ability to increase your energy levels, matcha offers a wide range of positive effects for overall well-being. In this chapter, we'll take a closer look at what makes matcha such a unique superfood and why it deserves a place in your daily routine.

BOOSTS ENERGY AND FOCUS

PEOPLE WHO REGULARLY CONSUME MATCHA GET A SENSE OF CALMNESS AND CLARITY, HELPING THEM FOCUS.

Matcha indeed contains caffeine. However, its effects differ significantly from those of coffee. Unlike coffee, which can cause sudden energy spikes followed by inevitable crashes, the caffeine in matcha provides a more stable energy that lasts longer. The reason for this is the presence of an amino acid called L-theanine. This amino acid has been shown to affect brain functions by improving mood, regulating sleep, and relieving stress disorders, making it easier to concentrate on daily tasks. This unique relationship between caffeine and L-theanine in matcha is what makes it a far superior choice to coffee for an extra boost of energy. Instead of feeling jittery and anxious, people who regularly consume matcha get a sense of calmness and clarity, helping them focus on their everyday lives. Whether you're working, studying, or simply going through your everyday routine, matcha can help you stay centered and efficient, making it a valuable addition to your daily routine.

SUPPORTS WEIGHT LOSS

MATCHA HAS AN EXTRAORDINARY ABILITY TO BOOST THE METABOLISM, HELPING YOUR BODY BURN FAT.

When it comes to weight loss, matcha should become your go-to option! It has an extraordinary ability to boost the metabolism, helping your body burn fat more effectively. The reason for this is a type of antioxidant called catechin—more specifically EGCG—which plays a crucial role in this process. Studies have shown that EGCG can ramp up fat oxidation during exercise, meaning it helps your body tap into those fat stores for energy when you're working out. In other words, starting your day with a warm cup of matcha tea or a latte can give your metabolism a little nudge and help those fats burn faster. Plus, these amino acids are crucial for balancing blood sugar levels and keeping those cravings in check. This way, a delicious cup of your preferred matcha drink will help you make healthier choices throughout the day. Whether you enjoy matcha as a soothing tea, a creamy latte, or even in a smoothie, you're giving your body some extra support in your weight-loss journey. After all, it's not just about losing that extra weight—it's about feeling great while doing it!

RICH IN ANTIOXIDANTS

MATCHA IS A FANTASTIC CHOICE TO BOOST YOUR PROTECTIVE MEASURES AGAINST OXIDATIVE STRESS AND INFLAMMATION.

Matcha is a powerful source of antioxidants, making it a valuable addition to a healthy diet. Antioxidants play a crucial role in fighting off free radicals in the body. These free radicals are unstable molecules that can be found everywhere, from environmental pollutants to foods we consume. They cause damage to our cells and contribute to chronic diseases. This is why having a strong defense is essential for our health.
What sets matcha apart from other types of green tea is its exceptionally high antioxidant content. In fact, matcha contains significantly more antioxidants than its green tea counterparts, making it a fantastic choice for those looking to boost their protective measures against oxidative stress and inflammation. This means that by incorporating matcha into your diet, you're not just enjoying a tasty beverage; you're also giving your body a powerful tool to combat potential health issues.
As mentioned above, the unique way matcha is grown and processed plays an important role in its high antioxidant level. Since matcha is made from shade-grown tea leaves, it develops a richer concentration of these protective compounds, making it a truly powerful tool in preventing many health issues and diseases.

DETOXIFIES THE BODY

A FASCINATING QUALITY OF MATCHA LIES IN ITS ABILITY TO CLEAN AND DETOXIFY OUR BODIES NATURALLY.

One of the most fascinating qualities of matcha lies in its ability to clean and detoxify our bodies naturally. This fantastic ability of matcha is due to its high chlorophyll content. Chlorophyll, the green pigment found in plants, plays a vital role in photosynthesis, but it also offers several health benefits when consumed. High levels of chlorophyll in matcha act as a natural binder of heavy metals and various other toxins that can accumulate in the body from environmental pollutants, processed foods, and even certain medications. When you drink matcha daily, the chlorophyll helps flush these harmful substances out of your system. As the body eliminates toxins, most people notice an improvement in their skin health and complexion.

Additionally, the detoxifying properties of matcha can contribute to better digestion. A healthier gut can lead to improved nutrient absorption and regularity, helping you feel lighter and more energized. Many people find that when their digestive system functions optimally, they experience less bloating, leading to overall improvement in well-being.

毎日の抹茶

MATCHA DAILY

With the obvious benefits matcha provides, you can greatly benefit from making matcha a part of your daily life. There are many ways to use matcha, and you can incorporate it into everything you do in the kitchen.

INCORPORATING MATCHA INTO YOUR DAILY ROUTINE

AS YOU WELL KNOW BY NOW, matcha's versatility goes beyond being a simple tea. A traditional preparation of matcha tea involves whisking the tea powder with hot water. However, matcha can also be incorporated into a wide variety of recipes.

In the following chapters, you'll find various matcha recipes you can easily incorporate into your daily menu. From fluffy matcha pancakes and muffins to savory dishes, I'm certain you will find something you like and can prepare for your loved ones.

For beginners, starting with a simple matcha tea or latte is an excellent introduction to the world of matcha. As you become more familiar with its unique taste and texture, you can explore other creative uses on your own, such as adding it to baked goods or savory dishes. The possibilities are truly endless, and matcha can easily be integrated into your diet, whether you're looking for a morning energy boost or a family dinner.

It is important to remember that matcha is much more than just a trendy beverage—it's a nutrient-packed superfood with a rich history and numerous health benefits. From its unique cultivation process to its impressive antioxidant content, matcha stands out as one of the most powerful and versatile ingredients you can incorporate into your daily routine. Whether you're seeking to improve your energy levels, enhance mental clarity, or simply enjoy a delicious and healthy drink, matcha offers something for everyone.

THE MATCHA RITUAL

How to Prepare Matcha Tea

The beauty of matcha lies in its preparation. Whether you're exploring the timeless Japanese tea ceremony or you prefer modern twists, such as iced matcha lattes, the process is an important part of the experience. In this chapter, we'll dive into how to make matcha, blending the rich traditions with easy, everyday methods that fit your lifestyle. Let's get started.

THE TRADITIONAL JAPANESE TEA CEREMONY

Matcha's Ceremonial Roots

AS MENTIONED EARLIER, matcha's origins are deeply intertwined with the Japanese tea ceremony. Chanoyu, or "the way of tea," has been practiced in Japan for over 800 years. The preparation and consumption of matcha in this context is more than just drinking tea—it's a meditative and artistic practice designed to create a moment of tranquility, harmony, and respect. The tea ceremony deepens the connection between host and guest, with each movement and gesture carefully considered and full of meaning. Traditionally performed in a quiet, minimalist tea room, the ceremony allows participants to slow down, focus on the present moment, and savor the simple act of making and drinking tea.

The traditional preparation begins with carefully cleaning each of these tools. After warming the chawan with hot water and then discarding the water, the host uses the chashaku to scoop two servings of matcha into the bowl. The temperature of the water is critical—around 80°C—to avoid burning the delicate tea. The host then pours the water over the matcha and begins to whisk using the chasen, holding it lightly and whisking in an "M" or "W" motion to create a smooth, frothy consistency.

This process may appear simple, but the attention to detail, rhythm, and flow of the ceremony make it an art form. Every step, from whisking to serving the tea, is performed with grace, respect, and mindfulness. In a world where life moves quickly, this ceremonial preparation invites you to slow down, focus on the present moment, and savor the sensory experience of matcha.

THE TOOLS

The tools used in the tea ceremony play a key role in making the perfect bowl of matcha, and they hold a special place in Japanese culture.

1. CHASEN
Bamboo whisk

Crafted from a single piece of bamboo, this whisk has multiple fine tines that help to mix the matcha powder with water, creating a smooth, frothy texture.

2. CHAWAN
Tea bowl

This ceramic bowl is used to mix and drink tea. It is often handmade, with no two bowls alike, making each one unique. The wide shape of the bowl allows for the perfect whisking of the tea.

3. CHASHAKU
Bamboo scoop

This is a small bamboo scoop used to transfer the matcha powder from its container into the bowl. It's used to measure the perfect amount of matcha—typically two scoops, which equals about 1–2 g of powder per serving.

4. NATSUME OR CHAIRE
Tea caddy

These are the containers used to hold matcha powder before it's prepared. They can range from simple to beautifully ornate, often showcasing detailed craftsmanship.

THE PHILOSOPHY BEHIND THE CEREMONY

THE JAPANESE TEA CEREMONY is rooted in Zen Buddhism, which emphasizes mindfulness, simplicity, and living in the present. By participating in a tea ceremony, one is not only enjoying a beverage but engaging in a spiritual practice. The ceremony teaches us to appreciate the beauty in simplicity and to find peace in everyday moments.

As part of this ritual, it's customary to take a moment of gratitude before drinking the tea, bowing in appreciation to the host. The first sip of matcha is often accompanied by a moment of quiet reflection as the tea drinker considers the texture, aroma, and flavor of the tea. This mindfulness extends to the physical senses—the warmth of the bowl in your hands, the soft aroma rising from the tea, and the vibrant green color.

EXPLORING MODERN MATCHA VARIATIONS

As matcha's popularity has surged beyond Japan, new variations of matcha drinks have emerged, offering tea lovers endless ways to enjoy this green tea powder. From refreshing iced matcha to indulgent matcha lattes and smoothies, these modern adaptations allow matcha to be enjoyed in a variety of contexts.

THE ART OF PERFECTING YOUR MATCHA

Whether you're preparing matcha traditionally or making a modern variation, there are a few key factors that will elevate your matcha-making experience. Understanding the nuances of water temperature, whisking techniques, and how to select high-quality matcha is essential to enjoying the best cup.

1

Water Temperature

One of the most important factors in making a delicious bowl of matcha is using the correct water temperature. Matcha's delicate leaves are sensitive to heat, and boiling water can scorch the powder, resulting in a bitter, unpleasant taste. For the best results, aim for water that's around 80°C. If you don't have a thermometer handy, simply boil water and let it sit for a minute or two before pouring it over your matcha.

2

Whisking for the Perfect Froth

The key to creating a smooth, frothy matcha is in the whisking. Traditional bamboo whisks, or chasen, are essential for this process. Hold the chasen lightly in your hand and whisk in an "M" or "W" motion, rather than a circular one, to incorporate air and create a creamy froth on top. For the best results, whisk quickly and vigorously. The finer the froth is, the better the matcha!

3

Choosing High-Quality Matcha

High-quality matcha is vibrant green and smooth in texture, indicating that the tea leaves were properly grown and harvested. Look for ceremonial-grade matcha, which is made from the youngest, most tender leaves and has a sweet, delicate flavor. Culinary-grade matcha is often more affordable but may have a stronger, more bitter taste, making it better suited for lattes or baked goods. The vibrant color of the powder is a good indicator of its quality; dull, yellowish matcha likely indicates a lower grade.

4

Proper Storage for Freshness

Matcha is delicate and can lose its flavor and color when exposed to air, light, or humidity. To ensure the best flavor, store matcha in an airtight container, preferably in the refrigerator. This will help preserve its freshness, color, and taste. Always make sure to consume your matcha within a few months of purchasing to ensure the best flavor experience. Matcha tends to degrade relatively quickly once opened, so using it within 1–2 months ensures you get the full benefits of its taste and nutrients.

抹茶の料理用途

CULINARY USES OF MATCHA

In this chapter, we'll take a look at how you can add matcha to all sorts of dishes, bringing not just great flavor but also a pop of color and a boost of nutrients.

SWEET CREATIONS

One of the most popular ways to use matcha in the kitchen is in sweet treats. It brings a one-of-a-kind flavor that adds a hint of bitterness, perfectly balancing out the sweetness in desserts. Plus, that vibrant green color really makes these goodies stand out!

Matcha Cakes and Cupcakes

Incorporating matcha into cakes and cupcakes creates desserts that are not only delicious but also visually striking. Whether mixed into a sponge cake batter or swirled into cream cheese frosting, matcha brings a mild, earthy flavor that complements the light sweetness of these desserts.

Matcha Cookies

Matcha also adds a fun twist to classic cookies. Adding it to shortbread or sugar cookie dough provides a subtle bitterness that pairs beautifully with the buttery richness of the cookie. Matcha shortbread is especially popular for its melt-in-your-mouth texture and slightly nutty finish.

Matcha Ice Cream and Puddings

Frozen treats, such as matcha ice cream, or soft, creamy puddings are great ways to enjoy matcha. The unique flavor of the tea gives you a nice balance that's both rich and refreshing—perfect for hot days or when you want something light for dessert!

When using matcha in sweet recipes, it's essential to select culinary-grade matcha, which is slightly more robust in flavor and more affordable than ceremonial-grade matcha. This ensures that the tea's flavor comes through without overpowering the dish.

MATCHA BEYOND SWEETS

While matcha is often associated with sweet treats, it also shines in savory dishes. Its unique quality makes it a versatile ingredient in various savory applications, adding complexity and depth to dishes.

Matcha Soups
Matcha can be incorporated into soups, especially creamy vegetable-based ones, where it acts as a flavor enhancer. Try whisking a small amount of matcha into a potato and leek soup or a creamy cauliflower soup for an earthy undertone that adds sophistication to the dish.

Matcha Dressings
Matcha also works well in dressings, providing a flavorful and visually appealing twist to salads. Mixing matcha into a basic vinaigrette or creamy dressing adds a touch of bitterness that pairs well with fresh greens, nuts, and fruits, bringing a new dimension to the salad.

Matcha in Marinades and Sauces
For a more adventurous use of matcha, try incorporating it into marinades or sauces. Matcha pairs particularly well with ingredients such as soy sauce, miso, and ginger, making it a perfect addition to an Asian-inspired marinade for grilled vegetables, tofu, or seafood.

CREATIVE MATCHA BEVERAGES

Beyond its role as a tea, matcha can be used to craft unique and exciting beverages that go beyond the traditional cup.

Matcha Smoothies
For a nutritious and energizing start to your day, add matcha to your morning smoothie. Its earthy flavor complements fruits such as banana, pineapple, and berries while also boosting the nutritional profile of the drink with antioxidants and a gentle caffeine kick.

Matcha Cocktails
Matcha is making its way into the world of cocktails, where bartenders are using it to create vibrant and refreshing drinks. Matcha pairs well with citrus, mint, and ginger, making it a great addition to cocktails such as mojitos or margaritas. A matcha gin sour, for example, combines the tea's bitterness with the crispness of gin and the tartness of lemon juice for a sophisticated and visually stunning cocktail.

Iced Matcha Lemonade
For a non-alcoholic option, iced matcha lemonade is a refreshing and simple drink that combines the tang of lemon with the rich, earthy notes of matcha. This beverage is perfect for hot days and provides a healthy alternative to sugary sodas or store-bought juices.

TIPS FOR SELECTING, STORING, AND USING MATCHA IN COOKING

To get the most out of matcha in your cooking, it's important to choose the right grade of matcha and store it properly to maintain its flavor and nutritional content.

Selecting Matcha
For culinary purposes, opt for culinary-grade matcha, which is less delicate than ceremonial-grade but still offers a vibrant color and flavor that works well in recipes.

Storing Matcha
Once opened, matcha should be stored in an airtight container, away from heat, light, and moisture. Refrigerating it can help preserve its freshness and prevent the powder from losing its vibrant green color and flavor over time.

Using Matcha in Recipes
When using matcha in recipes, it's best to sift the powder first to avoid clumping. This ensures a smooth texture and even distribution of flavor in your dish or beverage.

Whether you're experimenting with matcha in a cake, soup, or cocktail, the versatility of this green tea powder is undeniable. Its ability to enhance both the flavor and nutritional value of dishes makes it a must-have ingredient for any kitchen. By selecting high-quality matcha, storing it properly, and using it creatively in both sweet and savory recipes, you can bring the vibrant world of matcha into your culinary repertoire and enjoy its benefits beyond the traditional cup of tea.

カフェ

RECIPES

Now you know pretty much everything about matcha – now it's time to use matcha in the kitchen. Both as an ingredient in beverages, but also in baked goods, main dishes, and much more.

MATCHA GREEN TEA MUFFINS

12 | 15 min. | 18–20 min.

INGREDIENTS

1 cup whole wheat flour
½ cup oat flour *(or blend rolled oats in a blender until fine)*
¼ cup coconut sugar *(or your preferred sweetener)*
1 tablespoon matcha green tea powder
1 teaspoon baking powder
½ teaspoon baking soda
¼ teaspoon salt
½ cup unsweetened applesauce
¼ cup almond milk *(or any plant-based milk)*
¼ cup plain Greek yogurt *(or a non-dairy alternative)*
1 teaspoon vanilla extract
1 large egg *(or a flax egg for a vegan option)*

OPTIONAL ADD-INS

½ cup dark chocolate chips *(preferably 70% cacao or higher)*
½ cup chopped nuts *(such as walnuts or almonds)*
¼ cup dried fruit *(such as cranberries or raisins)*

INSTRUCTIONS

Preheat your oven to 180°C. Line a muffin tin with paper liners or grease it lightly.

In a large bowl, whisk together the whole wheat flour, oat flour, coconut sugar, matcha powder, baking powder, baking soda, and salt.

In another bowl, mix the applesauce, almond milk, Greek yogurt, vanilla extract, and egg until well combined.

Pour the wet ingredients into the dry ingredients and stir until just combined. Be careful not to overmix. If you're adding any optional ingredients, such as chocolate chips or nuts, fold them in gently.

Divide the batter evenly among the muffin cups, filling each about ⅔ full.

Bake in the preheated oven for 18–20 minutes or until a toothpick inserted in the center comes out clean.

Allow the muffins to cool in the pan for 5 minutes, then transfer them to a wire rack to cool completely.

MATCHA CHOCOLATE CHIP COOKIES

15 cookies | 15 min. | 10–12 min.

INGREDIENTS

1 cup whole wheat flour
½ cup almond flour *(or oat flour)*
1 tablespoon matcha green tea powder
½ teaspoon baking soda
¼ teaspoon salt
½ cup coconut sugar
(or a sugar substitute, such as stevia or monk fruit)
⅓ cup coconut oil, melted *(or unsalted butter)*
¼ cup maple syrup *(or honey)*
1 teaspoon vanilla extract
1 large egg *(or a flax egg for a vegan option)*
½ cup dark chocolate chips *(preferably 70% cacao or higher)*

OPTIONAL

¼ cup chopped nuts *(such as walnuts or pecans)*

INSTRUCTIONS

Preheat your oven to 180°C and line a baking sheet with parchment paper.

In a medium bowl, whisk together the whole wheat flour, almond flour, matcha powder, baking soda, salt, and coconut sugar.

In a separate bowl, mix the melted coconut oil, maple syrup, vanilla extract, and egg until well combined.

Pour the wet ingredients into the dry ingredients and stir until just combined. If you're adding chocolate chips and nuts, fold them in gently.

Scoop tablespoons of dough onto the prepared baking sheet, spacing them about 5 cm apart.

Bake for 10–12 minutes or until the edges are slightly golden. The cookies will firm up as they cool.

Let the cookies cool on the baking sheet for a few minutes before transferring them to a wire rack to cool completely. Enjoy your healthy matcha chocolate chip cookies!

MATCHA CHEESECAKE

8 | 15-20 min. | 35–40 min.

INGREDIENTS

FOR THE CRUST
1 cup almond flour
(or whole wheat flour)
¼ cup coconut oil, melted
(or unsalted butter)
2 tablespoons honey or maple syrup
¼ teaspoon salt

FOR THE CHEESECAKE FILLING
450 g cream cheese, softened
(use low-fat or Greek yogurt for a healthier option)
½ cup honey or maple syrup
(adjust for sweetness)
2 large eggs
2 tablespoons matcha green tea powder
1 teaspoon vanilla extract
1 tablespoon lemon juice
(optional, for brightness)

INSTRUCTIONS

Preheat your oven to 175°C. Grease a 22 cm springform pan or line it with parchment paper.

In a bowl, combine almond flour, melted coconut oil, honey (or maple syrup), and salt. Mix until crumbly.

Press the mixture into the bottom of the prepared pan to form an even crust.

Bake for about 10–12 minutes or until lightly golden. Remove from the oven and let it cool.

Meanwhile, in a large mixing bowl, beat the softened cream cheese until smooth.

Gradually add in the honey (or maple syrup) and mix until well combined.

Add the eggs one at a time, mixing well after each addition.

Add the matcha powder, vanilla extract, and lemon juice. Mix until smooth and fully combined.

Pour the matcha cheesecake filling over the cooled crust, spreading it evenly. Bake for 25–30 minutes, or until the edges are set but the center is slightly jiggly.

Allow the cheesecake to cool at room temperature for about an hour, then refrigerate for at least 4 hours or overnight to set completely.

Carefully remove the cheesecake from the springform pan. Slice and serve chilled.

SAVORY MATCHA PANCAKES

4 | 10 min. | 15–20 min.

INGREDIENTS

1 cup whole wheat flour *(or a gluten-free flour blend)*
1 tablespoon matcha green tea powder
1 teaspoon baking powder
½ teaspoon baking soda
¼ teaspoon salt
1 cup buttermilk *(or plant-based milk with 1 tablespoon of vinegar)*
1 large egg
1 tablespoon olive oil *(or melted coconut oil)*
¼ cup finely chopped green onions *(or chives)*
¼ cup grated cheese *(optional; use a low-fat cheese for a healthier option)*
Cooked vegetables *(such as spinach or zucchini; optional)*

INSTRUCTIONS

In a large bowl, whisk together the whole wheat flour, matcha powder, baking powder, baking soda, and salt.

In another bowl, mix the buttermilk, egg, and olive oil until combined.

Pour the wet ingredients into the dry ingredients and stir until just combined. Be careful not to overmix; it's okay if there are a few lumps.

Fold in the chopped green onions and any cooked vegetables or cheese, if using.

Heat a non-stick skillet or griddle over medium heat. Lightly grease with cooking spray or a small amount of oil.

Pour about ¼ cup of batter for each pancake onto the skillet. Cook for about 2–3 minutes until bubbles form on the surface.

Flip and cook for another 1–2 minutes until golden brown and cooked through.

Serve warm with a drizzle of olive oil or a dollop of Greek yogurt for added creaminess.

MATCHA OATMEAL

2 | 5 min. | 10 min.

INGREDIENTS

1 cup rolled oats
2 cups unsweetened almond milk *(or any milk of your choice)*
1 tablespoon matcha green tea powder
1 tablespoon maple syrup *(or honey; optional)*
¼ teaspoon vanilla extract
Pinch of salt
Toppings *(optional)*
sliced bananas, berries, nuts, seeds, or shredded coconut

INSTRUCTIONS

In a medium saucepan, combine the rolled oats, almond milk, and a pinch of salt. Bring to a boil over medium heat.

Reduce the heat to low and let the oats simmer for about 5–7 minutes, stirring occasionally, until they are creamy and cooked to your desired consistency.

In a small bowl, mix the matcha powder with a few tablespoons of hot water to create a smooth paste (this helps prevent clumping).

Once the oats are cooked, stir in the matcha paste, maple syrup, and vanilla extract. Mix well until everything is combined.

Pour the matcha oatmeal into bowls and top with your choice of sliced bananas, berries, nuts, seeds, or shredded coconut for added flavor and texture.

MATCHA CABBAGE SLAW

4 10 min.

INGREDIENTS

2 cups green cabbage, finely shredded
2 cups purple cabbage, finely shredded
1 large carrot, grated
2 tablespoons sesame seeds *(white or black)*

FOR THE MATCHA DRESSING

1 teaspoon matcha powder
3 tablespoons olive oil
1 tablespoon rice vinegar
1 tablespoon lemon juice
1 teaspoon honey (*or a low-carb alternative, such as stevia)*
1 teaspoon soy sauce *(or tamari for gluten-free)*
Salt and pepper, to taste

INSTRUCTIONS

In a large bowl, combine the shredded green and purple cabbage and grated carrot. Toss well to mix evenly.

In a separate bowl, whisk together the matcha powder, olive oil, rice vinegar, lemon juice, honey, soy sauce, salt, and pepper until smooth and well combined.

Pour the matcha dressing over the cabbage mixture and toss until the vegetables are well coated.

Sprinkle the sesame seeds on top and toss lightly once more.

Let the slaw sit for about 10 minutes to allow the flavors to meld, then serve fresh and enjoy!

MATCHA COCONUT ENERGY BITES

12 15 min.

INGREDIENTS

1 cup rolled oats
½ cup shredded coconut *(unsweetened)*
1/3 cup nut butter *(peanut, almond, or cashew)*
¼ cup honey or maple syrup *(for a vegan option)*
1 teaspoon matcha powder
1 tablespoon chia seeds *(optional for added texture)*
1 teaspoon vanilla extract
Pinch of salt
Extra shredded coconut for rolling *(optional)*

INSTRUCTIONS

In a large bowl, combine the oats, shredded coconut, matcha powder, and chia seeds (if using). Mix well.

In a small bowl, stir together the nut butter, honey or maple syrup, vanilla extract, and a pinch of salt until smooth and well combined.

Pour the wet ingredients into the dry ingredients and stir until everything is evenly mixed. The mixture should be sticky enough to form into balls; if it's too dry, add a bit more honey or nut butter.

Scoop out small portions (about a tablespoon each) and roll them into bite-sized balls using your hands.

If desired, roll the bites in extra shredded coconut to coat the outside.

Place the energy bites on a plate or in an airtight container and refrigerate for at least 20 minutes to firm up.

MATCHA FRUIT PARFAIT

2 10 min.

INGREDIENTS

1 cup plain Greek yogurt *(or any yogurt of your choice)*
1 teaspoon matcha powder
1 tablespoon honey *(plus extra for drizzling)*
½ teaspoon vanilla extract
½ cup granola
1 cup mixed fresh fruits *(such as berries, kiwi, mango, or bananas)*

INSTRUCTIONS

In a small bowl, mix the Greek yogurt, matcha powder, honey, and vanilla extract until smooth and well combined.

In serving glasses or bowls, layer 2 tablespoons of matcha yogurt at the bottom. Add a layer of fresh fruit, followed by a layer of granola.

Repeat the layers until the glasses are filled, finishing with a layer of fresh fruit on top. Drizzle a little extra honey over the top for sweetness.

Serve immediately.

MATCHA CHICKEN STIR-FRY

4 | 15 min. | 15 min.

INGREDIENTS

2 chicken breasts *(approximately 400 g)*, thinly sliced
1 tablespoon olive oil or sesame oil
1 red bell pepper, thinly sliced
1 medium zucchini, sliced into half-moons
1 medium carrot, julienned
1 cup broccoli florets
2 cloves garlic, minced
1 teaspoon fresh ginger, minced
2 green onions, chopped *(for garnish)*
Sesame seeds (for garnish)

FOR THE MATCHA SAUCE

1 teaspoon matcha powder
¼ cup soy sauce *(or tamari for gluten-free)*
2 tablespoons rice vinegar
1 tablespoon honey or maple syrup
1 tablespoon sesame oil
¼ cup water
Salt and pepper to taste

INSTRUCTIONS

In a small bowl, whisk together all the ingredients for the matcha sauce until smooth and well combined. Set aside.

Heat 1 tablespoon of olive oil or sesame oil in a large pan or wok over medium–high heat.

Add the sliced chicken to the pan and stir-fry for about 5–7 minutes, or until the chicken is fully cooked and slightly browned. Remove the chicken from the pan and set it aside.

In the same pan, add a bit more oil if needed, and sauté the garlic and ginger for 30 seconds until fragrant.

Add the red bell pepper, zucchini, carrot, and broccoli to the pan, and stir-fry for 4–5 minutes until the vegetables are tender-crisp.

Return the chicken to the pan, and pour the matcha sauce over the chicken and vegetables. Stir everything together, ensuring the sauce evenly coats the stir-fry.

Cook for an additional 2–3 minutes, allowing the flavors to meld and the sauce to slightly thicken.

Remove from heat and garnish with chopped green onions and sesame seeds.

MATCHA CHIA PUDDING

2

At least 3 hours

INGREDIENTS

1½ cups almond milk *(or any plant-based milk)*
2 tablespoons chia seeds
1 teaspoon matcha powder
1 tablespoon maple syrup or honey *(optional for sweetness)*
½ teaspoon vanilla extract
Fresh fruits *(such as berries, kiwi, or banana)* for topping
Nuts *(such as almonds, walnuts, or pistachios)* for topping

INSTRUCTIONS

In a medium bowl, whisk together the almond milk, matcha powder, maple syrup (if using), and vanilla extract until the matcha is fully dissolved and the mixture is smooth.

Add the chia seeds and stir well to combine. Make sure the chia seeds are evenly dispersed in the liquid.

Let the mixture sit for about 5–10 minutes, then give it another stir to prevent clumping.

Cover the bowl and refrigerate for at least 2–3 hours or overnight, allowing the chia seeds to expand and the pudding to thicken.

When ready to serve, give the pudding a quick stir and divide it into individual bowls or jars.

MATCHA SMOOTHIE BOWL

1 10 min.

INGREDIENTS

1 frozen banana
½ cup spinach *(fresh or frozen)*
1 teaspoon matcha powder
½ cup almond milk *(or any plant-based milk)*
1 tablespoon nut butter *(optional for creaminess)*

TOPPINGS
¼ cup granola
Fresh berries
(such as strawberries, blueberries, or raspberries)
Sliced banana
Chia seeds or shredded coconut *(optional)*

INSTRUCTIONS

In a blender, combine the frozen banana, spinach, matcha powder, almond milk, and nut butter (if using). Blend until smooth and creamy.

Pour the smoothie into a bowl and spread it evenly.

Top the smoothie with granola, fresh berries, sliced banana, and any additional toppings, such as chia seeds or shredded coconut.

Serve immediately and enjoy!

MATCHA SWEET POTATO MASH

4 | 15 min. | 25 min.

INGREDIENTS

2 large sweet potatoes, peeled and diced
1 teaspoon matcha powder
2 tablespoons olive oil or coconut oil
2 tablespoons almond milk *(or any milk of your choice)*
Salt and pepper, to taste

OPTIONAL TOPPINGS

Chopped green onions, sesame seeds, or crushed nuts

INSTRUCTIONS

In a large pot, bring salted water to a boil. Add the diced sweet potatoes and cook for about 15–20 minutes or until they are fork-tender.

Once cooked, drain the sweet potatoes, and return them to the pot.

Add the matcha powder, olive oil (or coconut oil), and almond milk to the sweet potatoes. Use a potato masher or fork to mash everything together until smooth and creamy.

Season with salt and pepper to taste. Adjust the consistency by adding more almond milk if necessary.

Transfer to a serving bowl and top with optional toppings such as chopped green onions, sesame seeds, or crushed nuts for added texture and flavor.

MATCHA HUMMUS

4 · 10 min.

INGREDIENTS

1 can *(425 g)* chickpeas, drained and rinsed
2 tablespoons tahini
1 tablespoon matcha powder
2 tablespoons olive oil
2 tablespoons lemon juice
1 clove garlic, minced
Salt and pepper, to taste
Water, as needed for consistency

OPTIONAL TOPPINGS

Sesame seeds, olive oil drizzle, or chopped herbs

INSTRUCTIONS

In a food processor, combine the chickpeas, tahini, matcha powder, olive oil, lemon juice, minced garlic, salt, and pepper.

Blend until smooth. If the mixture is too thick, add water one tablespoon at a time until the desired consistency is reached.

Taste the hummus and adjust the seasoning as needed, adding more salt, lemon juice, or garlic according to your preference.

Transfer the hummus to a serving bowl and drizzle with olive oil. Optionally, top with sesame seeds or chopped herbs for garnish.

Serve with fresh vegetables, whole-grain pita, or crackers.

MATCHA LATTE

1 | 5 min. | 5 min.

INGREDIENTS

1 teaspoon matcha powder
1 cup unsweetened almond milk
(or any plant-based milk of your choice)
1 tablespoon honey or maple syrup *(optional, for sweetness)*
½ teaspoon vanilla extract *(optional)*
A pinch of sea salt
Ice *(optional, for an iced version)*

INSTRUCTIONS

In a small bowl, sift the matcha powder to avoid clumps. Add a few tablespoons of hot water (not boiling—about 80°C) and whisk until smooth and frothy. A bamboo whisk works best, but you can also use a regular whisk or a frother.

In a saucepan, gently heat the almond milk over medium heat until warm. If you prefer a frothy latte, you can use a milk frother or blender to froth the milk.

In a large cup, combine the whisked matcha with the warm almond milk. Add honey or maple syrup, vanilla extract, and a pinch of sea salt. Stir well to combine.

Enjoy hot, or pour over ice for an iced matcha latte.

MATCHA INFUSED SALAD DRESSING

4 10 min.

INGREDIENTS

1 teaspoon matcha powder
3 tablespoons olive oil
2 tablespoons apple cider vinegar *(or rice vinegar)*
1 tablespoon honey or maple syrup *(optional for sweetness)*
1 teaspoon Dijon mustard *(optional)*
Salt and pepper to taste
1 tablespoon water *(to adjust consistency, if needed)*

INSTRUCTIONS

In a small bowl, whisk together the matcha powder and olive oil until well combined and smooth.

Add the apple cider vinegar, honey or maple syrup, and Dijon mustard. Whisk until the mixture is emulsified.

Season with salt and pepper to taste. If the dressing is too thick, add a tablespoon of water to reach your desired consistency.

Serve over your favorite salad or store in the refrigerator for up to a week.

CREAMY MATCHA BANANA SHAKE

1 | 5 min.

INGREDIENTS

1 ripe banana *(frozen for extra creaminess)*
1 cup unsweetened almond milk *(or any milk of your choice)*
1 teaspoon matcha powder
¼ cup Greek yogurt *(or coconut yogurt for a dairy-free option)*
1 tablespoon honey or maple syrup *(optional, to taste)*
½ teaspoon vanilla extract
Ice cubes *(optional, for a thicker texture)*

OPTIONAL

A few drops of mint extract for additional color and flavor

INSTRUCTIONS

In a blender, combine the frozen banana, almond milk, matcha powder, Greek yogurt, honey, and vanilla extract.

Blend until smooth and creamy. Add ice cubes if you'd like a thicker shake.

Taste and adjust sweetness if needed.

Pour into a glass and enjoy immediately. Optionally, garnish with fresh mint leaves, minced almonds, or your favorite berries.

OPTIONAL

Add a few drops of mint extract for a subtle minty flavor and a vibrant green hue. Blend briefly to incorporate.

MATCHA CREPES

4 | 10 min. | 15 min.

INGREDIENTS

¾ cup whole wheat flour *(or a 50:50 mix of whole wheat and all-purpose flour for a lighter texture)*
1 teaspoon matcha powder
1 tablespoon coconut sugar or your preferred sweetener
1/8 teaspoon salt
1 cup unsweetened almond milk *(or any milk of your choice)*
2 large eggs
1 teaspoon vanilla extract
1 tablespoon melted coconut oil or unsalted butter *(plus extra for greasing the pan)*

OPTIONAL TOPPINGS

Fresh strawberries
A dollop of whipped cream

INSTRUCTIONS

In a medium bowl, whisk together the flour, matcha powder, coconut sugar, and salt.

In another bowl, whisk the almond milk, eggs, vanilla extract, and melted coconut oil until smooth.

Gradually add the wet ingredients to the dry ingredients, whisking continuously to avoid lumps. Let the batter rest for 10–15 minutes.

Heat a non-stick skillet or crepe pan over medium heat and lightly grease with a bit of coconut oil or butter.

Pour about ¼ cup of batter into the pan, swirling it to coat the surface evenly.

Cook for 1-2 minutes, or until the edges start to lift and the bottom is lightly golden. Flip the crepe and cook for another 30 seconds to 1 minute.

Repeat with the remaining batter, greasing the pan as needed.

Stack the crepes on a plate and keep them warm. Serve with your choice of toppings and enjoy!

MATCHA DONUTS

6 | 10 min. | 12 min.

INGREDIENTS

1 cup whole wheat flour
1 teaspoon baking powder
¼ teaspoon baking soda
¼ teaspoon salt
1 tablespoon matcha powder
1/3 cup coconut sugar *(or your preferred sweetener)*
½ cup unsweetened almond milk *(or any milk of your choice)*
¼ cup plain Greek yogurt *(or coconut yogurt for a dairy-free option)*
2 tablespoons melted coconut oil *(or unsalted butter)*
1 teaspoon vanilla extract
1 large egg

OPTIONAL TOPPINGS

Fresh strawberries
Your favorite donut glaze

INSTRUCTIONS

Preheat your oven to 175°C. Grease a donut pan lightly with oil or non-stick spray.

In a medium bowl, whisk together the whole wheat flour, baking powder, baking soda, salt, matcha powder, and coconut sugar.

In another bowl, whisk the almond milk, Greek yogurt, melted coconut oil, vanilla extract, and egg until smooth.

Gradually add the wet ingredients to the dry ingredients, mixing just until combined. Avoid over mixing to keep the donuts fluffy.

Transfer the batter to a piping bag or use a spoon to fill the donut cavities about ¾ full. Bake for 10-12 minutes, or until a toothpick inserted into the center comes out clean. Let the donuts cool in the pan for 5 minutes, then transfer to a wire rack to cool completely.

OPTIONAL

serve with fresh strawberries and drizzle of your favorite donut glaze.

MATCHA ENERGY BARS

9

15 min.

INGREDIENTS

1 cup almonds
½ cup cashews
¼ cup sunflower seeds
¼ cup unsweetened coconut flakes
1 cup pitted dates *(softened if needed)*
2 tablespoons honey *(or maple syrup for a vegan option)*
1 teaspoon matcha powder

INSTRUCTIONS

If the dates are dry, soak them in warm water for 10 minutes, then drain.

Line an 20x20-cm pan with parchment paper for easy removal.

In a food processor, pulse the almonds, cashews, sunflower seeds, and coconut flakes until they are coarsely chopped. Set aside.

Add the dates, honey, and matcha powder to the food processor. Process until the mixture forms a sticky paste.

Add the chopped nut and seed mixture back into the food processor with the date paste.

Pulse until everything is well combined. The mixture should hold together when pressed.

Transfer the mixture to the prepared pan. Press it down firmly and evenly using your hands or the back of a spatula.

Refrigerate for at least 1 hour to set. Once firm, lift the mixture out of the pan using the parchment paper and cut it into bars or squares.

Store the bars in an airtight container in the refrigerator for up to 2 weeks or in the freezer for up to 3 months.

MATCHA LEMON AND LIME LEMONADE

2 · 5 min.

INGREDIENTS

2 cups water
1 teaspoon matcha powder
2 tablespoons hot water (for dissolving matcha)
Juice of 2 lemons (approximately 1⁄4 cup)
Juice of 2 limes (approximately 3 tablespoons)
2-3 tablespoons honey, maple syrup, or your preferred sweetener (to taste)
Ice cubes (for serving)

OPTIONAL GARNISH

Lemon or lime slices, mint leaves

INSTRUCTIONS

In a small bowl, whisk the matcha powder with 2 tablespoons of hot water until smooth and no clumps remain.

In a pitcher, combine the matcha mixture, lemon juice, lime juice, and sweetener. Stir until the sweetener is fully dissolved.

Pour in the 2 cups of water and stir to combine. Adjust sweetness and tartness to taste.

Fill glasses with ice and pour the matcha lemonade over the ice. Garnish with lemon or lime slices and mint leaves if desired.

ライフスタイル

KNOW YOUR MATCHA

It is important to buy and store your matcha correctly to get the full effect. In this chapter, you will learn how to identify high-quality matcha and how to handle it properly.

BUYING AND STORING MATCHA

When it comes to matcha, the quality of the powder you buy can make all the difference. But with so many options available, how do you know which type to choose? In this chapter, we'll explore the different grades of matcha, what sets them apart, and how to select the right one for your needs. We'll also talk about how to store matcha properly to keep it fresh so you can enjoy this beautiful green tea for longer.

Understanding the Grades

Matcha is typically divided into different grades based on its quality, and understanding these distinctions will help you make the right choice, whether you're planning to enjoy a traditional tea ceremony or experiment with culinary creations.

Ceremonial-Grade Matcha

At the top of the list is ceremonial-grade matcha. This is the highest quality available and is made from the youngest, most tender leaves from the top of the tea plant. As mentioned earlier, ceremonial-grade matcha is traditionally used in Japanese tea ceremonies and is meant to be enjoyed on its own, mixed only with water. The flavor is smooth, with a naturally sweet, earthy taste and a silky texture. The color is vibrant green, indicating a high level of chlorophyll and antioxidants.

If you're planning to drink matcha as a tea or savor it in its purest form, the ceremonial grade is your go-to. Although it is more expensive, the flavor and quality are unparalleled. It's worth the investment if you're looking for a refined matcha experience.

Culinary-Grade Matcha

Culinary-grade matcha is slightly lower in quality compared with ceremonial-grade, but it's still packed with flavor and nutrients. The leaves used for culinary matcha come from the lower parts of the tea plant and tend to have a slightly more bitter taste. This makes it ideal for blending into recipes where its natural bitterness can be balanced with other flavors, such as in smoothies, baked goods, or savory dishes.

Culinary-grade matcha is often more affordable than ceremonial-grade, and while it's not as delicate in flavor, it's still a great option for cooking and everyday use. If you're planning to incorporate matcha into your cooking or creative beverages, the culinary grade is perfect.

Lower-Quality Matcha

Finally, lower-quality matcha options are available, often labeled as "matcha blend" or "matcha powder." These can include fillers or be made from older leaves, resulting in a duller green color and a more pronounced bitterness. While these cheaper versions may be tempting, they usually lack the vibrant flavor and health benefits of higher-quality matcha.

UNION.P MATCHA CORNER
IMPORTED BY TEA MASTER
UJI · SHIZUOKA · NISHIO · YAME · KAGOSHIMA · KUMAMOTO
抹茶コーナー
UNION.P
COFFEE
BEST SELLER
RESTOCK SOON

HOW TO IDENTIFY HIGH-QUALITY MATCHA

Now that you know about the different grades, how can you tell if the matcha you're buying is high quality? There are a few key characteristics to look for

Color

High-quality matcha will be a bright, vibrant green. This indicates that the tea leaves were carefully shaded before harvest, allowing them to develop high levels of chlorophyll and antioxidants. If the matcha is more yellow or brown, it's likely lower in quality.

Texture

When you rub a bit of matcha between your fingers, it should feel smooth and almost silky, not grainy. The fine powder is a sign of careful processing, as the leaves are stone-ground to create a delicate, even texture.

Aroma

Good matcha should have a fresh, grassy aroma. If it smells stale or has little scent, it may be old or not stored properly. The fresher the aroma is, the better the flavor will be.

Origin

Matcha from Japan, particularly regions such as Uji, Kyoto, or Nishio, is known for its superior quality. These regions have ideal growing conditions and a long history of tea cultivation. Matcha from other countries may not adhere to the same stringent production methods, so it's worth looking for Japanese matcha if you're after the best.

STORING MATCHA

Matcha is incredibly delicate, and how you store it plays a huge role in maintaining its flavor and nutritional value. Once exposed to air, light, or heat, matcha can quickly lose its vibrant color and freshness. Here are some tips to help you store your matcha properly.

Airtight Containers

Matcha should always be stored in an airtight container to protect it from oxygen. Exposure to air can cause the powder to oxidize, which dulls its flavor and color over time. Many matcha brands come in resealable tins, but if yours doesn't, consider transferring it to an airtight jar after opening.

Keep it Cool

Heat is another enemy of matcha. To keep it fresh, store it in a cool place. Some people even store their matcha in the refrigerator to extend its shelf life. Just make sure the container is airtight and that the matcha doesn't absorb any moisture or odors from the fridge.

Avoid Light

Direct sunlight can degrade matcha quickly, so always store it in a dark place, such as a cupboard or pantry. If you do keep it in the fridge, be sure to wrap the container in a cloth or place it in an opaque container to block out light.

Use it Promptly

Matcha is best when it's fresh, so try to use it within a few months of opening. The longer it sits, the more its quality will decline, so don't be afraid to enjoy it frequently! If you're purchasing a large amount of matcha, consider buying smaller portions more regularly to ensure you're always using fresh powder.

Enjoy the full potential

Understanding the different grades of matcha and how to properly store it is key to enjoying its full potential in both flavor and health benefits. Whether you're using ceremonial-grade matcha for your daily tea ritual or culinary-grade matcha to whip up matcha-infused treats, choosing high-quality powder and storing it correctly will help you make the most of this ancient ingredient. By paying attention to its color, texture, and origin and taking steps to protect it from air, light, and heat, you'll be well on your way to becoming a matcha connoisseur!

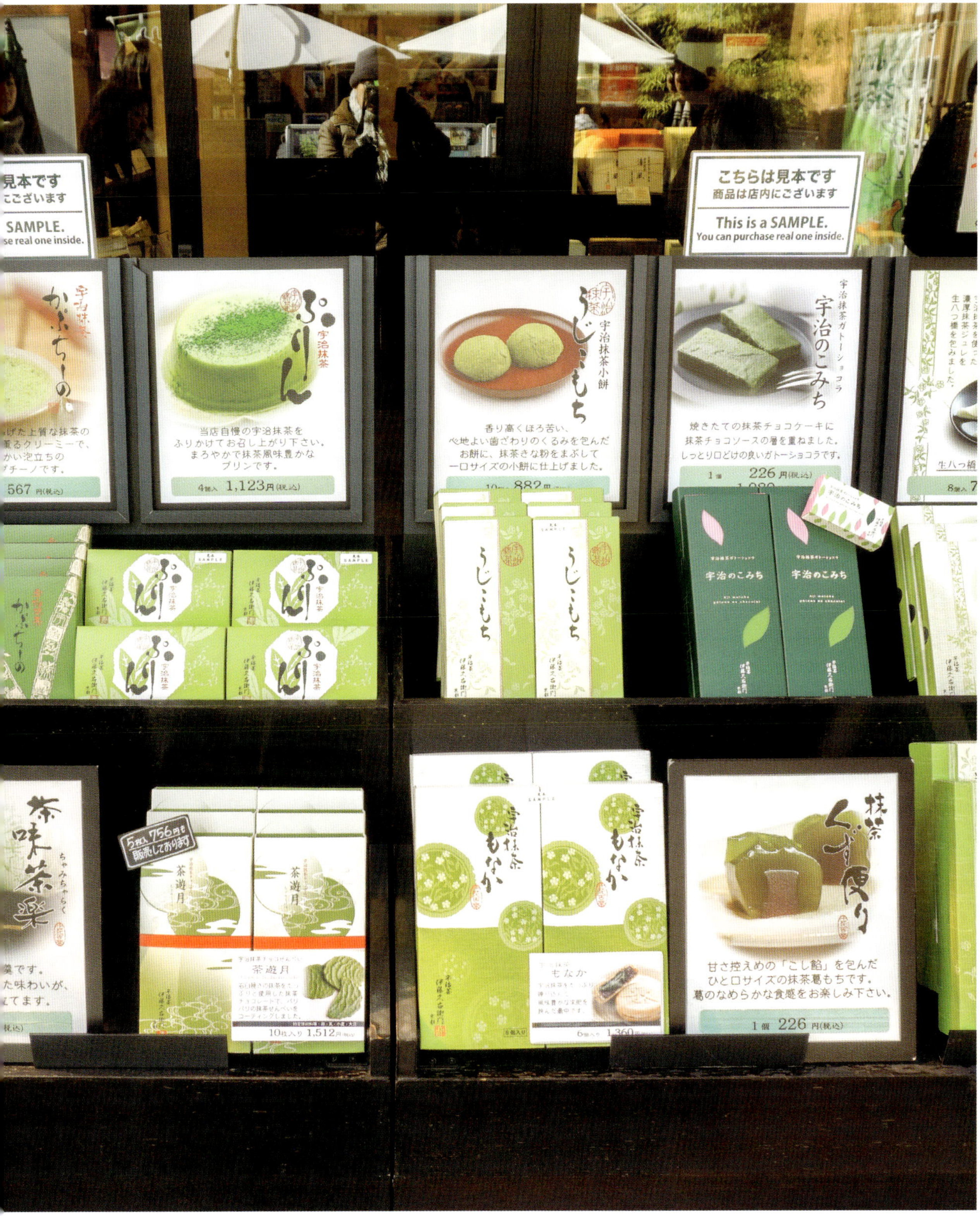
こちらは見本です
商品は店内にございます
This is a SAMPLE.
You can purchase real one inside.
宇治抹茶
ぷりん
当店自慢の宇治抹茶を
ふりかけてお召し上がり下さい。
まろやかで抹茶風味豊かな
プリンです。
4個入 1,123円(税込)
宇治抹茶小餅
うじこもち
香り高くほろ苦い、
心地よい歯ざわりのくるみを包んだ
お餅に、抹茶きな粉をまぶして
一口サイズの小餅に仕上げました。
宇治抹茶ガトーショコラ
宇治のこみち
焼きたての抹茶チョコケーキに
抹茶チョコソースの層を重ねました。
しっとり口どけの良いガトーショコラです。
1個 226円(税込)
宇治のこみち
5枚入 756円も
販売しております
茶遊月
10枚入り 1,512円
宇治抹茶
もなか
抹茶
くず便り
甘さ控えめの「こし餡」を包んだ
ひと口サイズの抹茶葛もちです。
葛のなめらかな食感をお楽しみ下さい。
1個 226円(税込)

MATCHA AS A LIFESTYLE CHOICE

As we explore the world of matcha, it becomes clear that it's not just a delightful beverage; it can be a transformative lifestyle choice. By incorporating matcha into your daily routine, you can enhance not only your physical health but also your mental and emotional well-being. In this chapter, we'll discuss practical ways to weave matcha into your life, highlighting its benefits beyond the cup.

MATCHA 24-7-365

Morning Matcha Rituals

Starting your day with a matcha latte can be a delightful way to awaken your senses. The gentle caffeine boost from matcha, combined with L-theanine, creates a calm energy that sets a positive tone for the day. As you well know by now, unlike coffee, matcha provides a sustained energy level without the rollercoaster effects.

You can prepare your morning matcha in various ways. Some prefer the traditional whisking method, mixing matcha powder with hot water until frothy. Others enjoy a creamier approach, blending matcha with almond milk or oat milk and adding a touch of honey or vanilla for sweetness. This morning ritual not only energizes your body but also gives you a moment of mindfulness to center yourself before diving into the day's activities.

Midday Energy Booster

As the afternoon slump rolls in, reaching for a matcha smoothie or a simple matcha tea can be an excellent way to revitalize your energy levels. Blending matcha with fruits, such as bananas, spinach, or avocados, can create a deliciously nutritious drink that fuels your body and mind. This is especially beneficial for those who experience mid-afternoon fatigue or need a pick-me-up during long work hours.

Additionally, matcha can be a powerful ally in managing stress. Its unique combination of caffeine and L-theanine promotes mental clarity while reducing anxiety, making it an ideal choice for those stressful moments. Consider keeping a jar of matcha powder at your workspace for easy access because a quick matcha break can offer a refreshing pause that enhances focus and productivity.

Evening Relaxation Rituals

Incorporating matcha into your evening routine can also be a soothing practice. While many may think of matcha strictly as a daytime drink, it can be just as enjoyable in the evening—especially when prepared as a warm latte with a touch of cinnamon or cardamom. These spices not only complement the flavor of matcha but also add their own health benefits, promoting digestion and relaxation.

Engaging in an evening matcha ritual can signal to your body that it's time to unwind. Pair your matcha with a few moments of quiet reflection or light stretching to create a calming atmosphere. This ritual can help ease the transition from the hustle and bustle of the day to a more peaceful state, enhancing your overall sense of well-being.

MENTAL CLARITY

Matcha is renowned for promoting mental clarity and focus. Unlike coffee, matcha reduces stress and anxiety, helping you stay alert and focused.

Matcha and Mental Clarity

Beyond its delicious flavor and versatility in recipes, matcha offers significant benefits for mental clarity. It can improve focus and concentration, making it a great companion during study sessions or creative work. Many matcha enthusiasts report feeling more alert and clear-headed after enjoying a cup, allowing for deeper engagement with the tasks at hand.

Moreover, matcha's rich antioxidant profile helps combat oxidative stress, which is linked to cognitive decline. By incorporating matcha into your daily routine, you can support not only your immediate mental performance but also long-term brain health.

Enhancing Emotional Well-Being

Adopting matcha as a lifestyle choice also emphasizes emotional well-being. The act of preparing and enjoying matcha can become a mindful practice, allowing you to take a break from the chaos of daily life. Mindfulness, in itself, is a powerful tool for reducing stress and enhancing emotional health. Taking the time to savor the aroma, color, and taste of matcha can create a moment of gratitude and presence, reminding you to slow down and appreciate the small joys.

A Holistic Approach to Health

Incorporating matcha into your life goes beyond just enjoying it as a drink; it's about taking a whole new approach to your health. Many people who love matcha notice that the values tied to it, such as mindfulness, balance, and wellness, start to influence other parts of their lives. This may mean eating more healthily, getting regular exercise, or finding ways to manage stress. Essentially, matcha can spark some positive changes in your lifestyle.

By viewing matcha as a lifestyle choice, you open yourself to a world of possibilities. It can inspire you to explore new recipes, engage in mindful practices, and foster a deeper connection with your health and well-being.

JENNIFER ANISTON

そして抹茶
有名人

CELEBRITIES AND MATCHA

Many celebrities greatly enjoy matcha, as it fits perfectly into their strong focus on health and the body.

GWYNETH PALTROW

MATCHA VIBE

As the founder of the lifestyle brand Goop, Gwyneth Paltrow has been at the forefront of the wellness movement, advocating for natural and holistic health solutions. She frequently discusses the benefits of matcha on Goop's platform, promoting it as a clean source of energy that avoids the crash associated with coffee.

DAILY RITUAL

Gwyneth often drinks matcha lattes made with almond or oat milk, sweetened naturally with ingredients like coconut or honey. Her matcha rituals are part of her broader approach to wellness, which includes clean eating, mindfulness, and fitness.

LACMA
GUCCI
ART+FILM
LACMA
ART+FILM
GUCCI
LACMA

KOURTNEY KARDASHIAN

MATCHA VIBE

Kourtney Kardashian has made matcha a staple in her life and frequently shares her favorite matcha latte recipes on her lifestyle website, Poosh. She often chooses organic, ceremonial-grade matcha and blends it with almond or coconut milk for a creamy, healthy drink.

DAILY RITUAL

Kourtney's matcha routine involves blending the green tea powder with a healthy fat, like coconut oil or ghee, which helps the body absorb matcha's antioxidants. She also sweetens it lightly with raw honey, making it a healthier, energizing drink.

MEGAN MARKLE

MATCHA VIBE

The Duchess of Sussex was a matcha enthusiast even before joining the British royal family. She used to post about her matcha latte routines on social media, particularly as a way to keep her energy up during her busy filming schedule.

DAILY RITUAL

Megan enjoys matcha for its sustained energy release and often drinks it as an alternative to coffee. She's been known to blend it with almond milk and add healthy sweeteners like honey.

usa

LADY GAGA

MATCHA VIBE

Lady Gaga's connection to matcha became prominent when she collaborated with Starbucks on a line of colorful, limited-edition drinks, including a "Matcha Lemonade," as part of her "Cups of Kindness" campaign.

DAILY RITUAL

While she might not be a daily matcha drinker, Gaga appreciates the unique flavors of matcha and uses it occasionally as a refreshing alternative to her other favorite beverages.

JENNIFER ANISTON

MATCHA VIBE

Jennifer Aniston is a wellness enthusiast who has been known to add matcha to her routine, preferring it over coffee for its health benefits and smoother energy release.

DAILY RITUAL

Aniston sometimes makes matcha lattes with almond or oat milk and may add a sprinkle of cinnamon or a touch of honey. She enjoys it for its antioxidants and uses it as a gentle way to stay energized throughout the day.

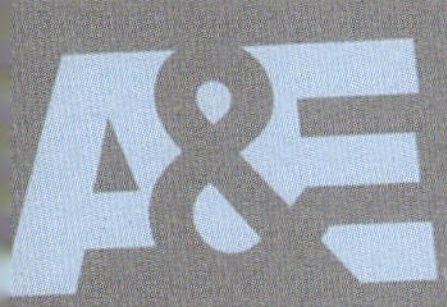

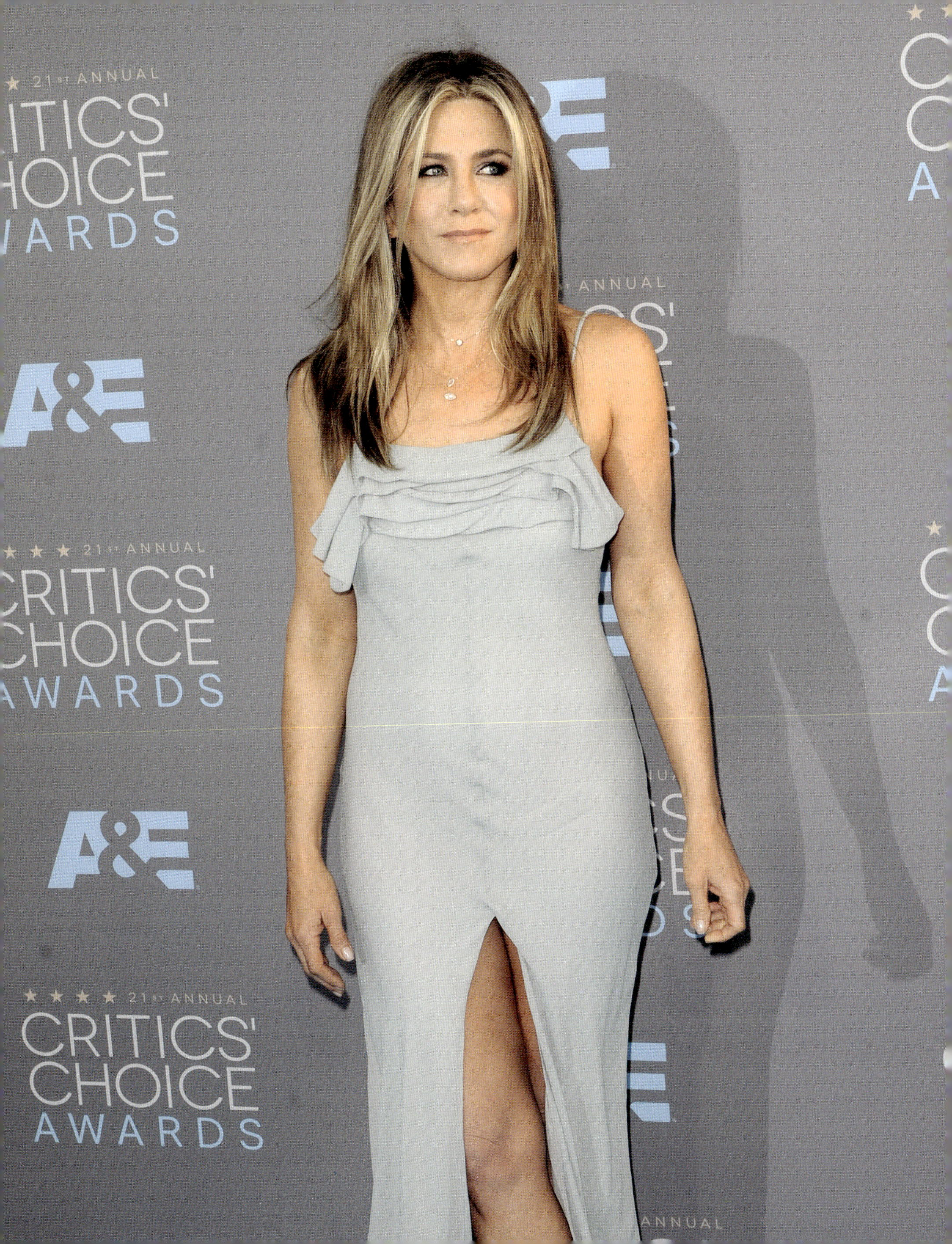
21ST ANNUAL
CRITICS'
CHOICE
AWARDS
A&E

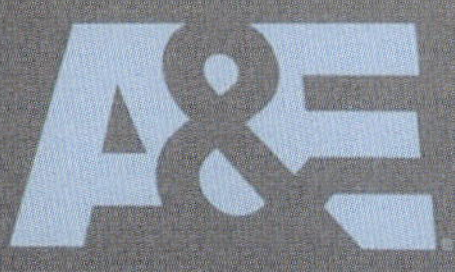

GQ
BRITISH
BOSS
HUGO BOSS

CHRIS HEMSWORTH

MATCHA VIBE

Known for his dedication to fitness and health, Chris Hemsworth has been open about his preference for matcha as a source of energy and antioxidants. He integrates it into his routine as a natural way to stay fueled and focused, especially during intense training for his roles.

DAILY RITUAL

Chris often drinks matcha lattes made with almond milk, pairing it with other superfoods or blending it into smoothies. His lifestyle app, Centr, even promotes matcha as part of its health and wellness recommendations.

MIRANDA KERR

MATCHA VIBE

Miranda Kerr, a supermodel and founder of Kora Organics, swears by matcha as part of her beauty and wellness regimen. She frequently drinks matcha lattes made with almond milk and a bit of coconut oil for added creaminess.

DAILY RITUAL

Miranda's routine includes matcha in the morning, often combined with superfoods like collagen powder for skin benefits. She believes it helps her stay energized and focused, while also nourishing her skin from within.

#QVC

SELENA GOMEZ

MATCHA VIBE

Selena has shared her love of matcha on social media and is occasionally seen with matcha lattes in hand, enjoying the drink as a calming part of her day.

DAILY RITUAL

Gomez prefers matcha for its calming and focus-enhancing effects. She often takes it as a latte with almond milk and a dash of cinnamon or honey.

DRAKE

MATCHA VIBE

The hip-hop artist and entrepreneur is known for his love of matcha. He frequently posts about his matcha drinks on social media and has been seen enjoying it as part of his everyday routine.

DAILY RITUAL

Drake often drinks matcha lattes, blending it with milk alternatives like oat or almond milk, and occasionally adding a sweetener. He also enjoys cold matcha drinks as a refreshing pick-me-up.

VICTORIA BECKHAM

MATCHA VIBE

Victoria Beckham frequently posts about matcha on her social media, highlighting it as part of her daily wellness routine. She's even shared photos of her favorite matcha brands and recipes with her followers.

DAILY RITUAL

Victoria typically drinks matcha with water or almond milk and enjoys it as a daily pick-me-up. She often chooses high-quality, ceremonial-grade matcha for its purer taste and benefits.

カ
フ
エ

CAFÉES

More and more cafés are specializing in matcha. We have traveled the world to find some of the best and most innovative places when it comes to using matcha on the menu.

INDONESIA

FEEL MATCHA

Feel Matcha is Indonesia's first locally established matcha café, renowned for offering an authentic matcha experience. Using premium 1st Grade Ceremonial Matcha sourced directly from Kyoto, Japan, the café ensures that every sip and bite reflects exceptional quality and taste.

The menu at Feel Matcha caters to matcha lovers with a variety of beverages and desserts. Highlights include their signature Matcha Latte, Matcha Salted Caramel Brulee, and Matcha Biscuit Lotus drinks. For dessert enthusiasts, they offer indulgent treats like Matcha Mille Crepe and Matcha Tiramisu, crafted to delight the palate with rich and creamy textures.

With multiple locations across Indonesia, Feel Matcha has become a hotspot for matcha aficionados.

Adress	Feel Matcha Jl. Kemang Timur No.47, RT.9/RW.3, Bangka, Kec. Mampang Prpt., Kota Jakarta Selatan, Daerah Khusus Ibukota Jakarta 12730, Indonesia
Opening hours	Everyday between 09:00-21:00.

MATCHA
Feel

Welcome いらっし

MALAYSIA

MUZI MATCHA

Muzi Matcha is a charming café located in Tambun, Ipoh, Malaysia, celebrated for its authentic Japanese-inspired atmosphere and a wide range of matcha-infused beverages and desserts. Situated in a beautifully designed bungalow, the café features a neat garden and expansive glass windows that flood the space with natural light, offering a serene and cozy ambiance.
Known for its delicious and affordable matcha creations, Muzi Matcha has become a favorite spot for matcha lovers. The café's interior reflects minimalist Japanese décor, enhancing its tranquil vibe and providing a relaxing setting for guests to enjoy their meals.

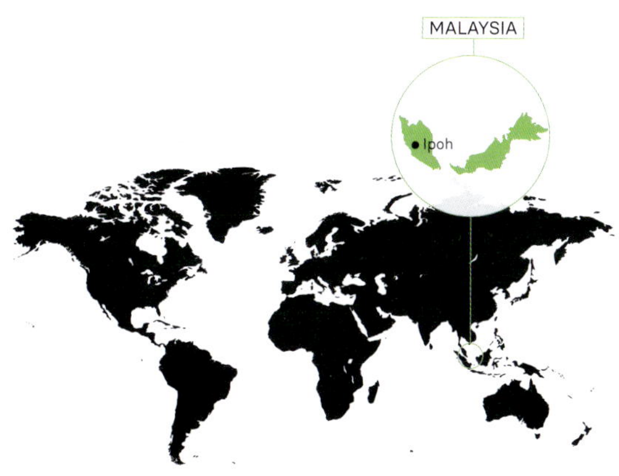

Adress	Muzi Matcha 333, Jalan Tambun, Kampung Tersusun Batu 5, 31400 Ipoh, Perak, Malaysia
Contact	+60 16-333 6520
Opening hours	Everyday 08-23

JAPAN

STARBUCKS RESERVE ROASTERY

The Starbucks Reserve Roastery Tokyo, located in the trendy Nakameguro district, is more than just a coffee shop—it's a multi-sensory experience where matcha meets cutting-edge design. Opened in 2019, this four-story architectural marvel combines Japan's love for tradition with modern innovation, offering an unparalleled journey into the world of tea and coffee.

Matcha lovers will find themselves in paradise at the Roastery. The Teavana Bar, located on the second floor, is dedicated entirely to tea, with matcha taking center stage. Here, visitors can enjoy ceremonial-grade matcha prepared in creative and flavorful ways.

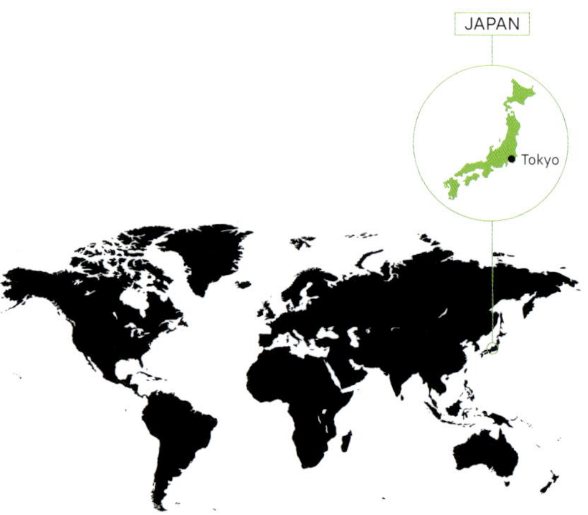

Adress	Starbucks Reserve Roastery 2 Chome-19-23 Aobadai, Meguro City, Tokyo 153-0042 Japan
Contact	+81364170202
Opening hours	sunday and monday: 07–22 tuesday – friday: 07–20 saturday: 07–22

359
MATCHAFUL
FARM-TO-WHISK
MAT
CHA
FUL
a matcha
wellness café

USA

MATCHAFUL

Matchaful, a female-founded café, has carved a niche in New York City by offering premium Japanese matcha and plant-based, gluten-free bites. Known for its dedication to sustainability and quality, Matchaful sources its matcha directly from multi-generational family farms in Japan, ensuring every cup reflects authenticity and care.

Matchaful's menu features an array of creative matcha-based drinks and light snacks, all crafted with organic ingredients and free from refined sugars.

Whether you're a matcha connoisseur or just starting your journey, Matchaful provides something for everyone.

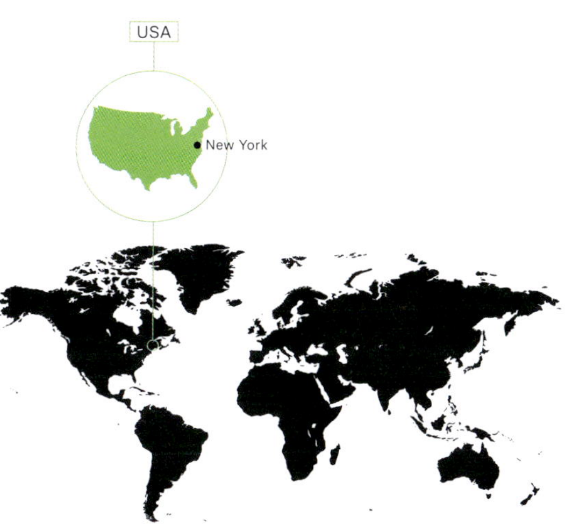

Adress	Matchaful 184 Prince St, New York, NY 10012, USA	
Contact	+16468961058	
Opening hours	saturday – tuesday:	09–16
	wednesday:	10–17
	tuesday – friday	08–18

THAILAND

OLNA CAFE

Nestled in the picturesque surroundings of Khao Yai, Olna Cafe offers a serene retreat with a charming European countryside vibe. While known for its idyllic setting and cozy ambiance, Olna Cafe has also become a destination for matcha enthusiasts, thanks to its diverse range of matcha-inspired beverages.

Olna Cafe elevates its matcha menu with high-quality ingredients and creative pairings, catering to both traditionalists and those looking for a modern twist.

To complement these beverages, Olna Cafe also serves a selection of matcha-infused desserts, such as matcha cheesecakes and pastries, crafted to pair perfectly with their drinks.

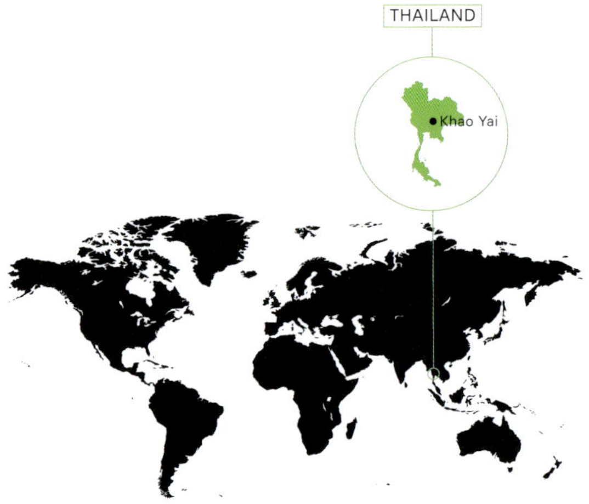

Adress	Olna Cafe 2213 Pak Chong District, Nakhon Ratchasima 30130	
Contact	+66650410835	
Opening hours	evryday between	08.30–17:00

mitsui garden hotel

BALI

MATCHA CAFE BALI

Matcha Cafe Bali, located in Canggu, is a haven for matcha enthusiasts seeking high-quality, organic matcha green tea beverages. Specializing in traditional and modern matcha creations, the café offers an array of matcha-based drinks, including lattes, smoothies, and ceremonial-grade matcha teas.

The menu extends the matcha experience into desserts and treats, featuring matcha-infused pancakes, cakes, and bowls. Known for its health-conscious ethos, the café ensures its offerings are vegan, gluten-free, and refined sugar-free where possible.

With its cozy ambiance and dedication to authentic matcha flavors, Matcha Cafe Bali has garnered rave reviews for delivering a true taste of this beloved Japanese tea in the heart of Bali. It's a must-visit for matcha lovers exploring the island.

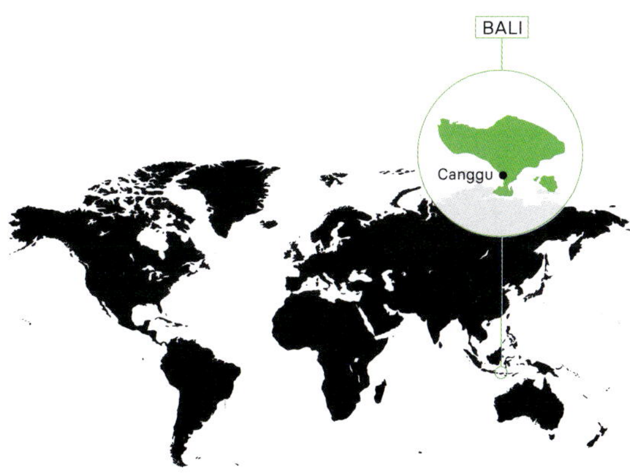

Adress	Matcha Cafe Bali Jl. Pantai Berawa No.99, Tibubeneng, Kec. Kuta Utara, Kabupaten Badung, Bali 80361, Indonesia
Contact	+62 812-3853-6138
Opening hours	Usually between 8-17

TAIWAN

MATCHA ONE

Matcha One, located in Taipei, is a matcha lover's paradise, celebrated for its dedication to authentic and high-quality Japanese matcha. This café specializes in showcasing the rich, nuanced flavors of premium matcha through expertly crafted beverages and desserts.

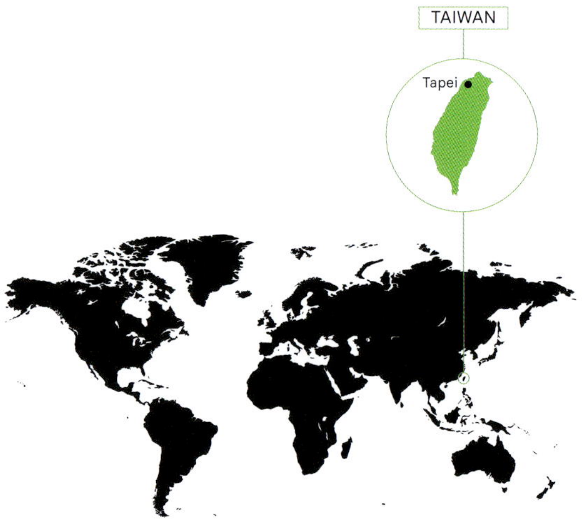

Adress	Matcha One No. 10, Lane 53, Qidong St, Zhongzheng District, Taipei City, Taiwan 100023
Contact	+886 2 2351 8181
Opening hours	Usually between 12-18:00. (Closed monday)

SPECIALTIES

HAND-WHISKED MATCHA

Experience the ceremonial essence of matcha with tea prepared using traditional Japanese techniques, highlighting its purity and depth.

MATCHA MILLE CREPE

A delicate dessert with multiple thin crepe layers interspersed with velvety matcha cream, perfectly balancing sweetness and the signature earthiness of matcha.

MATCHA MONT BLANC

A sophisticated treat combining matcha-infused chestnut puree, red bean paste, and matcha ice cream, designed for those who savor matcha's distinct bitterness and complexity.

MATCHA
ONE

JAPAN

NAKAJIMA-NO-OCHAYA

Nakajima-no-ochaya is a historic teahouse nestled within Tokyo's Hama-rikyu Gardens, offering a tranquil escape from the bustling city. Situated on a small island and connected by wooden bridges, it provides stunning views of the surrounding pond and beautifully manicured gardens.

The teahouse is renowned for its freshly whisked matcha green tea, which is traditionally served alongside seasonal wagashi, a type of Japanese confectionery. This pairing highlights the harmonious contrast between the tea's subtle bitterness and the sweetness of the treats. Guests can enjoy their refreshments while seated on traditional tatami mats indoors or on outdoor benches that

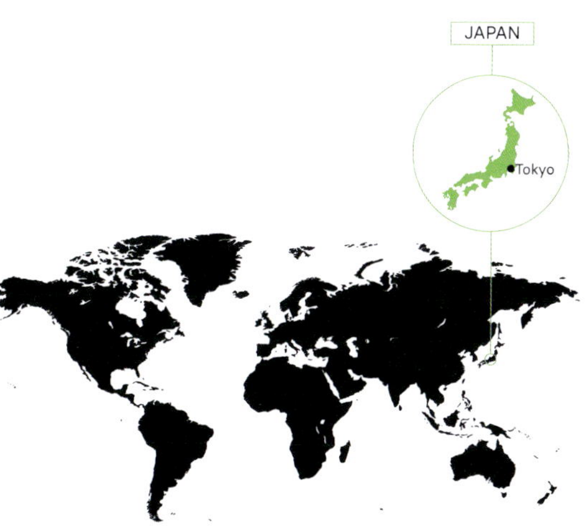

Adress	Nakajima-no-ochaya Japan, 1-1-1 Hamarikyu Gardens, Hamarikyuteien, Chuo-ku, Chuo City, 104-0046 Tokyo
Contact	+81335410200
Opening hours	Usually between 09-16:30

結
論

CONCLUSION

Matcha is amazing. You might already know that, and if not, you hopefully do after reading this book. The world of matcha has no limits, and matcha works for everything.

ENRICH YOUR LIVE

Health Benefits

We learned that matcha is packed with antioxidants, which can help combat oxidative stress and reduce the risk of chronic diseases. Its potential to support heart health, boost metabolism, and enhance cognitive function makes it a valuable addition to any diet.

Culinary Versatility

Matcha's vibrant green color and unique flavor profile can elevate both sweet and savory dishes. From matcha-infused cakes and cookies to savory soups and dressings, the possibilities are endless. We also discovered creative beverages beyond traditional tea, such as smoothies and cocktails, that showcase matcha's adaptability in the kitchen.

Buying and Storing Matcha

Understanding the different grades of matcha—ceremonial, culinary, and lower-quality options—equips you to make informed purchasing decisions. We discussed how to identify high-quality matcha by examining its color and aroma and offered practical storage tips to preserve its freshness and potency.

Integrating Matcha into Daily Life

We explored how to embrace matcha as a lifestyle choice, from morning rituals to midday boosts and evening relaxation practices. The mindfulness involved in preparing and consuming matcha can enhance your overall well-being and create moments of joy throughout your day.

YOUR HEALTH - YOUR BENEFIT

Now that you're armed with knowledge about matcha, it's time to take some steps toward embracing the "matcha life." Here are some practical ideas to help you get started

Start Your Day with Matcha
Incorporate a morning matcha latte into your routine. Experiment with different milks and sweeteners to find your perfect blend. Use this time for mindfulness, appreciating the aroma and flavors as you sip.

Culinary Exploration
Challenge yourself to incorporate matcha into your cooking. Try new recipes, from matcha pancakes to energy balls, and share your recipes with friends and family. You may just inspire others to adopt the matcha lifestyle!

Mindfulness Practices
Use matcha preparation as a moment for mindfulness. Set aside a few minutes each day to focus on the process, allowing it to be a calming ritual amidst the busyness of life.

Join the Community
Engage with fellow matcha enthusiasts through social media or local workshops. Sharing experiences and recipes can deepen your appreciation for matcha and inspire new ideas.

IN SYNC WITH MATCHA

Embracing matcha as part of your daily life is more than just enjoying a tasty drink; it's a commitment to enhancing your overall quality of life.

FROM MORNING RITUALS that kickstart your day to calming evening practices that help you wind down, matcha offers countless ways to nurture your body and mind. By integrating matcha into your routines and viewing it as a holistic tool for well-being, you can cultivate a lifestyle that celebrates health, mindfulness, and joy.

With each sip, you're not just indulging in a delicious beverage—you're also inviting a moment of tranquility into your day. Matcha encourages you to slow down and appreciate the present, making it a perfect companion for mindfulness practices. Plus, as you explore different matcha recipes and preparation methods, you'll discover a whole new world of flavors and experiences that enrich your everyday diet. So, whether you're sipping a vibrant matcha latte, blending a refreshing smoothie, or enjoying a soothing evening cup, let matcha be your partner on this journey toward a healthier, more balanced life.

CREDITS

Front page	jcomp	Freepik.com
Page 2		Freepik.com
Page 4	Miguel Tamayo Fotografia	Shutterstock.com
Page 7	Azra Hodza	
Page 8	Petr Brezina	Shutterstock.com
Page 10	7maru	Shutterstock.com
Page 13	Petr Brezina	Shutterstock.com
Page 14	Light Stock	Shutterstock.com
Page 17	Nishihama	Shutterstock.com
Page 18	Nishihama	Shutterstock.com
Page 20	DRG Photography	Shutterstock.com
Page 23	gyn9037	shutterstock.com
Page 24	Uber Bilder	Alamy
Page 25	Yuri A	Shutterstock
Page 26	Andriy Blokhin	Shutterstock.com
Page 27	Azra Hodza	
Page 28	wirestock	Freepik.com
Page 31	ST Line Art	Freepik.com
Page 32	xbudhong	Freepik.com
Page 33	awpixel.com	Freepik.com
Page 34	ST Line Art	Freepik.com
Page 34	Ritamarni0506	Freepik.com
Page 35	ST Line Art	Freepik.com
Page 36	ST Line Art	Freepik.com
Page 37	ST Line Art	Freepik.com
Page 38		Freepik.com
Page 41	pvproductions	Freepik.com
Page 42	ZOE	Unsplash.com
Page 45	jovan-vasiljevic	Unsplash.com
Page 46	Monika Grabkowska	Unsplash.com
Page 49	Tatiana Buzmakova	Shutterstock.com
Page 51	Rosa Sepanta	Unsplash.com
Page 52	Shayna Douglas	Unsplash.com
Page 54	PeopleImages.com - Yuri A	Shutterstock.com
Page 55		Freepik.com
Page 56	Japan_room	Shutterstock.com
Page 57	May Lawrence	Unsplash.com
Page 59	pangjaikanyawee	Freepik.com
Page 60	Nattapat.J	Shutterstock.com
Page 63	Azra Hodza	

Page 64	Azra Hodza	
Page 67	Azra Hodza	
Page 68	Image Professionals GmbH	Alamy Stock Photo
Page 70	Azra Hodza	
Page 112	Fengianum	Shutterstock.com
Page 115	Opasbbb	Shutterstock.com
Page 116		Freepik.com
Page 119	Atiwat Witthayanurut	Shutterstock.com
Page 121	Unstoppable Art	Shutterstock.com
Page 122	Ground Picture	Shutterstock.com
Page 123	Natakie Sysko	Unsplash.com
Page 123		Freepik.com
Page 125		Freepik.com
Page 126	Walter Cicchetti	Shutterstock.com
Page 129	Andrea Raffin	Shutterstock.com
Page 130	Eugene Powers	Shutterstock.com
Page 133	Ovidiu Hrubaru	Shutterstock.com
Page 134	Tinseltown	Shutterstock.com
Page 137	Tinseltown	Shutterstock.com
Page 138	Featureflash Photo Agency	Shutterstock.com
Page 141	Featureflash Photo Agency	Shutterstock.com
Page 142	Tinseltown	Shutterstock.com
Page 145	Jgphotographydetroit	Shutterstock.com
Page 146	Featureflash Photo Agency	Shutterstock.com
Page 148	Alana Harris	Unsplash.com
Page 151	Luna A. Safitri	Shutterstock.com
Page 152	jamesteohart	Shutterstock.com
Page 155	yu_photo	Shutterstock.com
Page 156.	Robert K. Chin - Storefronts	Alamy Stock Photo
Page 159		Shutterstock.com
Page 160	Kuremo	Shutterstock.com
Page 162	Syifa Elfina	Shutterstock.com
Page 162	Cheedman007	Freepik.com
Page 162	mrsiraphol	freepik.com
Page 164	ReiKlaus	Shutterstock.com
Page 166	zakiroff2000	Freepik.com
Page 169		Freepik.com
Page 170		Freepik.com
Page 173	Japan_room	Shutterstock.com

MATCHA

Text and recipe photos: Azra Hodza
Editor: Jesper Helmin
Bookdesign and layout: butter am brot = Morten Svendsen

ISBN: 978-87-94190-86-2
1. edition, 2. print run

Printet at Print Best, Estonia, 2025

For the past 15 years, Azra has been crafting and capturing the art of food. Her expertise spans healthy, visually appealing, and affordable recipes, ensuring that indulgence and nutrition go hand in hand. She has authored and contributed to various cookbooks, focusing on weight loss, health, and creative twists on classic dishes.

Helmin Publishing
Nivå Strandpark 21
DK-2990 Nivå
Denmark
helminpublishing.dk